WHERE SHOULD WE HAVE STOPPED?

WHERE SHOULD WE HAVE STOPPED?

The Story of a Remarkable Family

Fred Behringer

iUniverse, Inc.
Bloomington

Where Should We Have Stopped?
The Story of a Remarkable Family

iUniverse books may be ordered through booksellers or by contacting:

iUniverse
1663 Liberty Drive
Bloomington, IN 47403
www.iuniverse.com
1-800-Authors (1-800-288-4677)

Because of the dynamic nature of the Internet, any web addresses or links contained in this book may have changed since publication and may no longer be valid. The views expressed in this work are solely those of the author and do not necessarily reflect the views of the publisher, and the publisher hereby disclaims any responsibility for them.

The front cover photo shows the Walsh family trimming a Christmas tree at the Haverford Hotel in suburban Philadelphia in 1964. The Main Line Times photo by Bill Harris was the first full-color image published by the newspaper. Reproduced with permission.

The back cover photo shows Bill and Barbara Walsh at the celebration of their 60th wedding anniversary at Skytop Lodge in 2008. Photo by V.I.P. Studios, Inc., Ken Schurman. Reproduced with permission.

ISBN: 978-1-4759-3231-7 (sc)
ISBN: 978-1-4759-3233-1 (hc)
ISBN: 978-1-4759-3232-4 (e)

Printed in the United States of America

iUniverse rev. date: 07/12/2012

Dedicated to Barbara S. Walsh

CONTENTS

1. A Wonderful Priest? 3

2. The Years at Villanova 6

3. Service in the Navy 8

4. Law Student Meets Model 11

5. How to Keep from Starving 14

6. Plainfield to Philadelphia 17

7. Taking Time to Dance 25

8. Swimmin' Walsh Women 29

9. Booth Lane Memories. 34

10. A Letter to the Children 40

11. Bill Responds to 9-11 47

12. Growing Up "Walsh" 49

13. Barbara's "the Glue" 55

14. Eagles, Warriors and Wildcats. 57

15. Meet the Children. 60

16. Everyone Is Different 79

17. Retreating to Malvern 87

18. Bill and the Knights 93

19. Bill's View on Religion 96

20. Loyalty to Villanova 98

21. "Service Above Self" 100

22. Thoughts from Friends 105

23. The Walsh Open 110

24. Golfing in Florida 116

25. Special Mother's Day Gift 118

26. Gentlemen in Red Blazers 120

27. Adventures in Ireland 122

28. 50,000 Golf Balls and Counting 128

29. Augusta National – No. 500 131

30. The "Raiders" and the "Whites" 135

31. Business Organizations 141

32. The American College 146

33. The J. Wood Platt Trust 151

34. A Leading Role with GAP 155

35. Not Cheaper by the Dozen 158

36. A Very Enjoyable Dinner Partner 161

INTRODUCTION

I t didn't take long for teachers to project a career path for young Bill Walsh. Sister Mary Edward at St. Francis Grammar School in Metuchen, New Jersey was the first to conclude: "William, you'll make a wonderful priest." It was a refrain Bill heard throughout his Catholic upbringing. "When you were educated in Catholic schools and were an obedient kid with pretty good marks, the nuns picked you out as a good prospect to be a priest," he recalled. "And in our generation, whatever priests or nuns told us we accepted as gospel, so I began to think that I was destined to be a priest."

That possibility remained in Bill's mind even through his college years. He did not carry an overwhelming feeling that "God was telling me what to do," but he showed little serious interest in girls. "I thought if I'm going to be a priest, why get tangled up with them?" Then during his last semester in college, Bill would travel home on weekends clad in his impressive Navy V12 uniform, and he noticed girls on the train were looking at him, "maybe even flirting." After he caught the attention of attractive young ladies a few other times, "I began to realize that maybe I didn't want to be a priest, but if I'm not going to be a priest, I've got to make sure I find a girl who wants to have children, because to be a good Catholic, I've got to have 10 children."

Beginning Law School at the University of Pennsylvania in September 1946, Bill kept an eye out for a girl who shared that child-raising ambition.

In December of 1947, a good friend and fellow law student, Bob Lindsey, proclaimed, "Walsh, I have just the girl for you. She's a good Catholic who goes to Mass every day, and she wants 10 children." He introduced Bill to Barbara Straub a few weeks later, and they were wed less than a year later.

Bill was so anxious to get their large family underway that when Barbara wasn't pregnant six weeks after they were married, he said to her in all seriousness, "Do you think we ought to see a doctor to see if anything is wrong with either of us?" Barbara wisely cautioned patience, and soon she was pregnant. Bill feels no husband was ever happier than he when their first child, Stephanie, was born on August 12, 1949.

The birth of Alexandra Walsh on January 23, 1968 meant Bill and Barbara had exceeded their family goal by five. They feel blessed to have raised 15 healthy children, all outstanding individuals in their own right.

"About the only negative thought I had with so many children was how much it cost," Bill said, "particularly when they started going to college. But neither of us ever regretted having the children we did."

Talking at the couple's 60th wedding anniversary celebration, Bill told the children, "If we had shopped for a family before we were married, we couldn't have been luckier than to find the Walsh family. Some people questioned raising such a big family, but I would look around the room and ask all of you, 'Where should we have stopped?' " Meaning, of course, that some very special people might not have joined the family.

CHAPTER 1

A Wonderful Priest?

William Thomas Walsh was born on March 23, 1922, to William Earl and Gladys French Walsh in Westfield, New Jersey, a small town of about 8,000 people about 25 miles southeast of New York City in Union County. For 10 years, the family lived in a three-bedroom house on West Dudley Avenue in what Bill describes as a "nice town that is still a class place today."

Because Holy Trinity Catholic School was a mile away, Bill and his younger sister, Joan, went to Roosevelt Grammar School for first and second grade. For third and fourth grade, they went to Holy Trinity. Then with a growing family, the Walshes moved to a seven-bedroom farmhouse on three acres in Metuchen, New Jersey (sisters Patricia and Sheila had arrived.) To Bill's ongoing consternation, two acres of the property contained grass that required constant mowing—and mowing was Bill's job, one that took all day, using a push mower or a gas mower that often stalled. Yet this labor resulted in an important lesson that carried through Bill's life: "My father said that's a big job when you start out, but if you just keep going around in those circles, you'll find that the circle becomes much smaller. You'll find that out about all jobs in life, that they look so big in the beginning, but if you just start out on them with the right attitude, you get to the point where it's a breeze to the end. And that's true in paperwork, in reading or anything like that. You get started, plunge in, and it becomes manageable."

Tackling another chore at home brought Bill to the brink of disaster when he attempted to paint the house without a ladder tall enough to reach the highest points. "I decided to put two step ladders together with a big board across them and then put a ladder on top of that. I got up on it and everything seemed fine, but when I stretched to reach one of the little eaves with a paintbrush, everything collapsed. I'm up three floors right under the roof, and I landed in an evergreen bush, so I was really fortunate. I could have killed myself, broken an arm, broken a leg, ruined my back, but God was taking care of me, I guess."

In Metuchen, Bill went to St. Francis Grammar School, where fifth and sixth grades formed one class, taught by Sister Mary Edward, who rarely smiled and kept order with a ruler. Bill's ever-present smiles and laughter caused the nun to label him a "wise-acre," but he did so well in his early tests that she quickly promoted him from fifth grade into sixth. "This was looked upon as an honor by the school and my parents," Bill recalls, "but it turned out to probably have hurt me. I became the youngest, smallest and most naïve person in the graduating class in eighth and 12th grades." In the eighth grade, he placed first in his class academically.

At five foot, two inches and 98 pounds entering St. Peter's High School in New Brunswick, Bill struggled to overcome his diminutive stature as he tried out for sports teams. He played football and baseball but missed the cut in basketball. A thrilling 7-0 victory in football over the New Brunswick High School freshmen stands out in his memory, as does a stop he made by driving a blocker into a ball carrier so forcefully that the runner was flipped into the air. "The cheers from the crowd were the most I ever had as a kid." The St. Peter's varsity coach told Bill, "We're waiting for you next year, Red," but Bill's father would not let him continue with football. He joined the boxing team, continued with baseball and worked at a bowling alley in New Brunswick, where he once recorded a score of 257.

More significantly for his future, Bill became a caddie at Metuchen

Golf and Country Club and received a junior membership at the club as a birthday gift. He soon signaled a special aptitude for the game of golf, which he first played with his grandfather as a 10-year-old at Galloping Hill Golf Course. Showing his incredible memory of details from childhood on, Bill recalls scoring 68-64–132 for his first 18 holes. "My grandfather counted every stroke."

Caddies could play every Monday at Metuchen so Bill would play as many as 54 holes once a week. He convinced the principal at St. Peter's to let him skip the graduation ceremony to play the final match for the Metuchen Junior Club Championship, which he won on the 34th hole with an eagle.

Bill graduated in the top 10 of his high school class and impressed his senior homeroom teacher, who echoed Sister Mary Edward's feeling: "William, you'll make a wonderful priest."

CHAPTER 2

The Years at Villanova

In September 1939, Bill took his father's advice to get work experience before going to college, becoming an office boy at Milbank, Tweed, Hope & Webb, a large law firm in New York City. He earned $15 a week less 15 cents for Social Security. "Essentially we were gofers delivering large manila envelopes. If the delivery point was 23 blocks or more, we were given a nickel for the subway. Unless it was 40 blocks or more, some of us would keep the nickel and walk very fast or run so that we were back in normal time." As we'll learn, Bill resumed running long distances later in life. Lunch at the Horn and Hardart Automat was soup, chicken potpie and water for 25 cents, also presaging a habit of Bill's not to spend money extravagantly.

Meanwhile, Bill and his parents were ruminating about where he would attend college. Bill leaned toward the University of Notre Dame, but his father said, "In New York it's thought of primarily as an athletic school." His father favored the University of Pennsylvania's Wharton School, but after Bill's year of working in Manhattan, he wanted to get away from the city atmosphere. His mother liked Princeton University, but Bill thought it was too close to home. They settled on Villanova College (now Villanova University) in suburban Philadelphia with a large campus in a country setting. Selecting a Catholic school tied in with Bill's lingering notion that he might become a priest.

Thus in September 1940, Bill began a love affair with Villanova that has continued throughout his life. He hit the books hard from the beginning and ranked sixth in his class after the first semester, while finding time for a full schedule of sports and activities. Then 5 foot, 10 inches tall and weighing 140 pounds, he tried out for the basketball team but was cut by the renowned coach Al Severance. "He was very nice to me, but I deserved to be cut. He had many prospects much better than I was." Bill found his niche on the golf team, playing number one while winning six of nine matches, equaling the team's record. He improved to seven wins and two losses as a sophomore, ending his college golf career since Villanova dropped golf because of World War II.

Bill also played basketball for his fraternity team and broke the intramural record with 35 points in a game. Later he played centerfield for the baseball team and served as sports editor of the student newspaper and yearbook. He maintained high grades throughout his stay at Villanova and received a medal for finishing first academically in the Commerce and Finance School. Villanova also honored him for taking part in the most extra-curricular activities for the four years.

After a slow start, Bill's social life picked up while at Villanova as thoughts of the priesthood receded from his mind. "There weren't any female students at Villanova in those days," Bill said, "and I was too bashful to ask anyone out from Rosement, a girls' college less than a mile away. I was told by an upper classman that if you didn't go to the Sophomore Hop, you were really looked down upon. I said that I didn't know any girls but if he could get me a date with Pat Kennedy (the sister of future President Kennedy and the future Mrs. Peter Lawford), who was a student at Rosemont, I would go. He arranged it, and so I went. She was very nice, tall and a good dancer, and we had an enjoyable time. I had one more date with her at dinner, but she indicated she was going to transfer to Stanford, which she did, and I never saw her again."

In the meantime, the Walsh family added two more children, David and Colleen. Because he was not living at home, Bill didn't really get to know them until he arrived back home in mid 1946.

CHAPTER 3

Service in the Navy

With World War II raging, Bill enrolled in the U.S. Navy V-1 program (later V-12) in May of 1942 with the guarantee that he could finish college before going on active duty. That summer he worked in brutal heat for 83 cents an hour scraping paint off gasoline storage tanks at the E.I. DuPont de Nemours plant in Grasselli, New Jersey. He managed to get on the golf course occasionally, winning a club championship at Metuchen, and he caddied at the prestigious Merion Golf Club, not far from Villanova.

Bill learned a little about the cost of a social life on a date with Rosemary Convery, a student at a Holy Child school in Philadelphia, who lived with her parents in West Philadelphia. The check for dinner and dancing at Jack Walton's Roof on top of the Hotel Walton came to $42.50 (there's his memory of details again), and Bill had $45—"every cent I owned"—with him. He left $1.50 for the waiter, spent his last dollar to take Rosemary home on public transportation and walked from West Philadelphia to Villanova, arriving at 2:30 a.m. "Can you imagine," he says now, "walking on Lancaster Avenue for two and a half hours at that hour these days without being shot or robbed?"

Rosemary was Bill's partner at another memorable dinner when they met Bill Heavey, a friend from Villanova, and his fiancée at the Hotel Pennsylvania in New York City. They danced to the music of Frankie Carle and his orchestra, and Carle sat at the table next to them after each break in the music, joined by legendary bandleader Glenn Miller and his wife. Miller, who was in uniform, told them he was leaving to entertain troops in France the next morning. His plane disappeared over the English Channel, and his body was never found. "This was a great shock to all four of us," Bill remembers. "His orchestra was my favorite. I still have recordings of his renditions of the most popular songs of the day."

Bill had traveled to New York for that date from Harvard, where he was on a pass from the Naval Supply Corps School based at the Harvard Business School Campus. He was part of an elite Navy V-12 group selected for the school, which would lead to commission as an ensign. Bill graduated on May 15, 1944, and was ordered to Camp Bradford, Virginia, near Norfolk, a training site for landing ships. There Bill met Barbara Rhea, a freshman at Chestnut Hill College, whose father was a captain in the Navy, and for the first time he felt he was getting interested in a girl. He even traveled to Florida to meet her parents, but the relationship cooled when they realized Bill wasn't interested in a permanent naval career.

On January 2, 1945, Bill reported to New Orleans to board LSM 330, a medium-sized landing ship, and departed for the Panama Canal, passed through the canal and went on to San Francisco and subsequently to Hawaii, Guadalcanal, the Philippines, Guam and Saipan. Serving as disbursement officer for as many as 25 ships, Bill had to transport as much as $650,000 in cash. LSM 330 was ordered in late July 1945 to prepare to take part in the invasion of Japan, but in early August, he recalls, "The atom bombs were dropped on Nagasaki and Hiroshima, and everything came to a halt."

The war was ending, but Bill's service in the Navy continued until September 1946 in the Philippines and later in New York City, permitting him once again to commute from Metuchen. By then, he had decided to attend law school and gained acceptance to the schools at Columbia, Cornell and the University of Pennsylvania. He chose Penn.

Before he started law school on September 4, 1946, Bill found time to resume golf at Metuchen and tied the course record of 66. "I was winning money on most of the days I played, and it was very enjoyable to be playing again, not only for the game itself but also for the renewed friendships I was enjoying."

CHAPTER 4

Law Student Meets Model

A professor told Bill and 158 other first-year students at the Penn Law School to "look to both sides of you because one-third of you will not make it to the second year." Bill advanced, but only 103 of the students who started were still with him. "My marks were pretty good—in the upper 25 percent of the class. I must say that Law School was much tougher than college or Midshipman School, and I felt fortunate to have done that well."

Bill was also fortunate to draw a seat assignment next to Bob Lindsey, who knew of Bill's goal of 10 children. The Law School students attracted numerous invitations to dances at Penn sororities, and Bill dated eight of the girls he met at the dances. Not bashful about his future plans, he asked each of the eight how many children they would like to have. The answers ranged from zero to two. "That was not very encouraging. I never dated any of them again, and I'm sure they thought I was some kind of nut who had somehow been admitted by the Law School."

Enter Bob Lindsey with word that he found "just the girl for Bill." Barbara Straub grew up in Oil City, Pennsylvania, with six siblings: Kathy, Marty, Nancy, Bill, Dick and Jane. She had graduated from Georgetown Visitation Convent in Washington, D.C. and was working as a fashion model at leading department stores in Philadelphia, including Bonwit Teller, Lit Brothers, Strawbridge & Clothier and Gimbels. Lindsey introduced her to Bill in December of 1947. "She was beautiful and a lovely young lady of 19," said Bill, who then was 25. "I could hardly wait until our first date so that I could learn more about her. On our first date in January 1948, we had a very enjoyable time talking about the joys of growing up in a large family. She was one of seven children, and I had five younger brothers and sisters. We talked, I recall, about how many children we wanted to have."

One date led to another, and Bill took Barbara to meet his family in April. "I admire Bill's choice very much," said his father. His grandmother fulfilled a longstanding promise by giving Bill her engagement ring, saying, "Billy, you have to get engaged to her. You can't leave her out there where someone else might propose to her." Bill and Barbara became engaged on April 26, 1948.

The year of their engagement, Gimbels selected Barbara as the Cathedral Bride for the store's annual bridal show. She remembers, "I was so excited that they invited me to be the top model who was in the most important gown in the most important part of the show." And Bill was excited to be in the audience.

Their wedding took place September 17, 1948. Proceeding from their first date to the wedding in less than a year seemed to be rushing things, as Barbara looks back today: "I think now how lucky we are. That could have been a disaster. We both basically came from the same backgrounds and the same religion. I think all of that made it easier. When people get married, you have to make adjustments to her way of life, his way of life and what's going to be our way of life, whether it's how you celebrate Christmas or how you celebrate birthdays. You have to do your own thing. I think because we both came from similar situations, the adjustments were not huge."

Although they both wanted a large family, Barbara says with emphasis, "We married because we were in love. I wasn't going to get married until I was 28 or 30 years old. I was having a nice career, and then when I met Bill, it was like, boy, I fell hook, line and sinker very quickly. I think the fact that I had never really loved anybody before, it was very obvious to me that he was the right one."

Bill received his law degree in February 1949. While still in law school, he started selling life insurance part time to help make ends meet, not realizing the future career significance of that venture. With a government subsidy for a returning veteran, the couple lived on $300 a month since Barbara discontinued modeling after her fifth month of pregnancy. They moved from West Philadelphia to Plainfield, New Jersey, where Bill secured a clerkship with a Union County District Court judge in order to qualify for the New Jersey Bar exam. And he continued to sell insurance at night while practicing law during the day.

Bill's golf career also was progressing as winnings from matches helped pay the bills, although he particularly remembers one match where all the money went to fighting polio. Four leading male and female amateurs competed at Metuchen Golf Club as mixed pairs, Bill teaming with Mrs. William Tracy. "We started out well and were leading after the first nine holes. I was just playing along, concentrating on the competition and didn't realize I was out in 32, four under par, until one of the spectators told me. The news apparently spread around the course as our gallery swelled by the 11th hole. Even Barbara, eight and one-half months pregnant, was brought out to watch. Somehow I ended up with another 32 for a total of 64, a stroke below the course record. Our team won the tournament, and each of us received a beautiful woolen blanket and many plaudits." The *New Brunswick Daily Home News* headline credited the course record to "Billy Walsh, gangling 22-year-old youth," although Walsh was 27 at the time.

Two weeks later, Barbara gave birth to the first of 15 Walsh children, Stephanie, on August 12, 1949. The new parent remembers feeling overwhelmed, thinking, "I'm completely responsible for the life of this new baby. The responsibility absolutely blew my mind." And Bill notes, "Although this important part of our lives interfered with our sleep, our schedules and with our lives in general, we never had second thoughts about continuing to want 10 children."

CHAPTER 5

How to Keep from Starving

Bill endeavored to establish his law practice in 1950 while continuing to sell life insurance at night. "I was still quite optimistic about the law prospects as I had a few potentially lucrative clients." One was the inventor of an automobile shock absorber touted as better than anything on the market. He approached Bill to find him a financial backer so he could start production. The trouble was that during two meetings with the inventor, he refused to give any information about the product, simply insisting that it would be the best. "I spent a lot of time and received nothing in the way of income. I vowed I would do my best to avoid inventors in the future."

Another lesson occurred when the mayor of Plainfield offered Bill $35 to represent a client of his who was in the city jail on charges of passing bad checks. Bill endured an uncomfortable visit to the jailhouse where he interviewed the client and received a lecture from a judge who felt Bill should have been aware that the client faced more serious charges in another county. However, Bill managed to get the bad-check charges dropped. "While I was naturally very pleased that the case had been decided as it was, I determined that I wouldn't take any more criminal cases. I just didn't feel right about defending someone I believed was guilty."

Bill continued to perform well on the golf course in 1950, winning the Union County Bar Association Championship at Baltusrol Golf Club, one of the most highly regarded clubs in the country.

1950 also marked the birth of the Walshes' second child, Pamela, on November 12. Her older sister, Stephie, had trouble pronouncing the new baby's name, calling her "Pamina," which developed into "Minna," the nickname that followed her through school and into adult life.

If Bill's legal career was not flourishing, his insurance career took a significant step forward when he was offered the position of district manager of the Equitable Life Assurance Society, with a guaranteed income of $10,000 in the first year, more than twice what Bill was earning as a lawyer and salesman. Howard Petith, the agency manager, told Bill, "I've looked over this agency very closely, and I've come to the conclusion that you're the only young person in it who has any hope of being a success. I know you went through law school and all the rigors of the bar exam, but I also know you must be starving to death." Bill was concerned about his father's reaction if he concentrated on selling insurance "because he was so proud of my being a lawyer." And he was not certain he could make a living in sales. After long discussions with Barbara, Bill accepted the offer contingent on his succeeding in a forthcoming sales campaign. He placed first in the agency, won a trip to Washington, D.C. and took the job, doing his best to humor his father.

"Everything went well. I was fortunate to recruit some very good people, and my earnings in the first 12 months were $12,464, exceeding my guarantee by $2,464 and making me feel I had definitely made the right decision. Even my father reluctantly agreed." Thus Bill's law career pretty much came to a close as he set out on the path that turned out so well.

And the family continued to grow. Barbara gave birth to Bridget on July 29, 1952, thrilling Bill, although he asked himself, "When are the boys going to start?"

In 1953, Bill and Barbara moved from an apartment to a rented house in Plainfield. After borrowing Bill's grandfather's 1931 Nash to get around, the judge for whom Bill had clerked sold them his 1950 Studebaker, telling Bill he needed a nicer car to get ahead in business. His district was doing well, and Bill passed the final exam to earn the Chartered Life Underwriter designation.

On July 25, 1953, Barbara gave birth to Monica, the couple's fourth daughter.

CHAPTER 6

Plainfield to Philadelphia

While the family was growing and the insurance business was increasing, golf also claimed a significant share of Bill's time and attention. His team's victory in the 1953 Plainfield Area League Championship earned team members and their wives a celebratory dinner arranged by Dominic Toresco of Toresco Motors, the team's sponsor. "I had never experienced an Italian dinner before—seven courses of excellent food, and it lasted two and a half hours," Bill remembers. "We were still talking about it 10 years later."

The golf league matches took place at Plainfield West, a public course related to the neighboring Plainfield Country Club, which boasts a nationally ranked course designed by the famous Donald Ross. Every time Bill passed the Ross course, he said to himself, "Someday, I'll be a member there."

Frank O'Brien, a good friend with whom Bill had played in tournaments and a Plainfield member, encouraged Bill to consider joining the club, but Bill was hesitant. "My main concern was that this was where the Plainfield elite belonged, and here I was, a young lawyer-turned-life insurance manager who didn't feel he yet belonged. Frank kept telling me, 'With a golf game like yours and the education you have, you don't have to have a lot of money. I'll guarantee that I can get you in,' which he did in early 1954." Bill borrowed $900 from a life insurance policy to pay the dues and initiation fee. Plainfield Country Club became an important part of Bill's life, a connection that continues to this day.

Bill added to his golf achievements in 1954 as he reached the semi-finals of the club championship and won the Plainfield City Championship for all clubs in the Plainfield area. He and O'Brien reached the finals of the New Jersey Better Ball Championship. And his Equitable Life district continued to lead the agency in sales campaigns.

But 1954 saw an even more significant event for the Walshes—the birth of Michael, their first son, on October 18.

Bill continued in 1955 to push his district staff to top ranking because he wanted to be an agency manager. His team not only led the agency in the April campaign but placed high in the New York Metropolitan area, earning Bill an invitation to speak to the New York district managers. "Now a lot more people knew who I was."

On August 1, Howard Petith and Joe Beasley, the Equitable Life sales vice president, summoned Bill to the home office for an interview about becoming an agency manager in Philadelphia. "What wonderful news! If I were to be promoted, other than staying in New Jersey, Philadelphia was the next best place. The interview went well, and it was agreed that I would start in Philadelphia on September 1, 1955. Because Barbara was again pregnant, she stayed in New Jersey while Bill lived at the Drake Hotel when he began his new job. Their sixth child and fifth daughter, Therese ("Tez") was born on September 22, 1955.

When the couple rented a six-bedroom house in Bala Cynwyd, Lower Merion Township, moving the family and belongings from New Jersey became an adventure, starting with a snowstorm that delayed the moving truck by a day. Meanwhile, the children came down with chicken pox. The family had to spend a night in the Haverford Hotel after sneaking the children past the front desk. There wasn't much sleep that night, and the next day offered no relaxation as the moving truck arrived. The new baby missed the excitement because Bill and Barbara left her at a children's nursing home in Plainfield for a few weeks.

The insurance agency manager Bill replaced, Melville P. Dickenson, became Group Insurance vice president at the home office. Dickenson, a member of Pine Valley Golf Club, generally regarded as the greatest golf course in the world, recommended membership in Pine Valley to Bill. Two of the agents reporting to Bill were Woody Platt and Bill Hyndman, who became two of the best players in Philadelphia golf history. They were accustomed to playing rounds at Pine Valley, Dickenson told Bill, and they would need a host. Bill had already been proposed as a member at Philadelphia Country Club, however, and did not feel he could afford a second club. He promised Dickenson he would seriously consider the invitation at a later time, and he did.

Bill had left the office in Cranford, New Jersey in excellent hands. One of his sales recruits, Jay Mikula, succeeded him as district manager and eventually became a vice president in the home office, as did another recruit, Bob Keating. Recruits Bill Nebb, Ray Sheelen and Joe Hyman all went on to successful careers with Equitable, and two other recruits became successful managers with other companies.

An important benefit of Bill's promotion was attendance at the annual managers' meeting, usually held at the beautiful Boca Raton Hotel in Florida. When they arrived for the January 1956 meeting, the regal, palm-lined entrance suggested to Bill and Barbara that they were somewhere special. "After the first evening's cocktail party and dinner, the dancing to Freddie Martin's Orchestra in the moonlight under the stars, and the excellent service and cuisine," Bill said, "we found out that it certainly was a very special place."

That first evening, one of the older managers whom Bill had met when he spoke in New York City—apparently enjoying the cocktails—looked across the table at Bill and Barbara and said with a serious expression, "Walsh, I think you over-married." Bill laughed and replied, "I agree with you." He recalls, "Barbara did look stunning, as she always did at important affairs, and I was flattered."

Bill liked the makeup of his agency staff, including Mel Dickenson Jr., the son of the manager he replaced; Ted Brod and Ed Steele as district managers; Dick Scott, Mike Paider and Bill Robinson as sales recruits.

"The growth wasn't as fast or as large as I would like to have seen, but it wasn't bad, and the existing older agents, including the famous golfers Woody Platt and Bill Hyndman, seemed to be pleased with what we were trying to accomplish and were most cooperative in anything I asked them to do." In 1955 Platt won the first United States Golf Association Senior Amateur Championship, and Hyndman reached the finals of the U.S. Amateur Championship.

The possibility of Pine Valley membership surfaced again in August of 1956, when Mel Dickenson Jr. invited Bill to play in the club's Member-Guest Championship. They reached the finals of the Championship Flight but lost on the 19th hole when one of their opponents made a 50-foot putt. "While drowning our sorrows at the bar, Mel Jr. talked me into filling out a membership application for Pine Valley." As we shall see, it was a momentous decision.

At Philadelphia Country Club, Bill won his first—but certainly not his last—club championship. And at Plainfield, where Bill had continued his membership, he lost in the finals of the club championship to his friend Frank O'Brien.

Bill and Barbara welcomed their sixth daughter and seventh child, Hilary ("Huddie"), on November 2, 1956. To provide more space for the growing family, they bought a house in St. Davids on the Main Line in suburban Philadelphia. "It was a much more comfortable house with more lawn and far less traffic than we had before."

Bill and Barbara started in their third year of marriage to go out for dinner, mostly by themselves, one night a week, usually Friday. A regular baby-sitter would come in, feed the children and get them ready for bed. Bill and Barbara would then be home before they went to sleep—usually between 8 and 8:30.

"As the children got older," said Bill, "we would tell them that this was our 'date night,' and they kidded us about it, but we feel they appreciated our still being enough in love to have a 'date' each week. In the big picture, we feel that it had a lot to do with how the children not only realized how much

we loved them but also how much we loved each other. At least they still talk about it."

Barbara explained, "When you have that many children around, you don't get much time together. Bill worked really hard, and he worked long hours, and being in the life insurance business, he had to work at night. He'd come home for dinner, and then turn around and go out again."

Their daughter Bridget remembers, "Their standing date was the Covered Wagon Inn in Strafford for dinner on Friday night. They knew all the help there. Dad was always a great tipper, and everybody loved to wait on them. It was their opportunity to go out and reconnect with each other and sort of catch up and remind themselves they had a marriage in addition to all these children. My mom had always advised young people getting married to maintain your relationship because you two were together before the children were."

Huddie said she learned from Bill and Barbara "that the strength of their relationship made it possible for them to love each of us. I know from my own experience with seven children how difficult it can be to get untangled from kids' commitments and to spend time alone together."

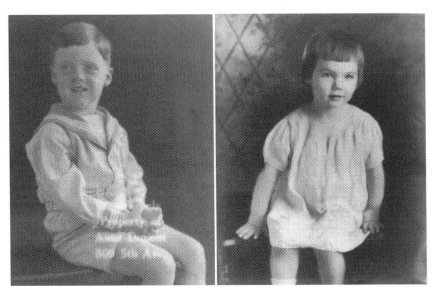

Bill and Barbara at an early age.

Bill and Barbara as high school seniors.

The home in Metuchen, New Jersey, where Bill
spent so many hours cutting the grass.

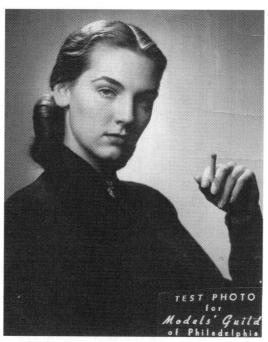

TEST PHOTO
for
Models' Guild
of Philadelphia

Barbara was one of the leading fashion models in Philadelphia at
a time when posing with a cigarette was not frowned upon.

Bill was in U.S. Navy garb when he graduated
from Villanova in the Class of 1943.

Bill and Barbara were married on September 17, 1948.

CHAPTER 7

Taking Time to Dance

B ill's insurance sales in 1955 qualified him for the Million Dollar Round Table. This did not mean he earned $1 million, as some people thought, but it did confirm that his sales of permanent life insurance for the year exceeded $1 million. "While not too many managers spent much time selling, and the company didn't push it, I personally not only needed the income but also felt that I could be a better leader of the agency by showing that I could sell and thereby lead by example." Bill often accompanied his sales people on calls, giving all of the commissions from any sales from these calls to new recruits and half the commissions to experienced agents.

It was fortunate that Bill's sales efforts were succeeding, because the cost of raising the family was steadily increasing in the late 1950s and early 1960s. The couple's second son, Matthew, arrived January 6, 1958, followed by Timothy on April 9, 1959; Daniel (the biggest baby at 10 pounds, four ounces) on August 19, 1960; Maura on October 31, 1961; and Brendan on December 26, 1962 (his mother's birth date). Now there were seven girls and five boys.

"Barbara and I really hadn't thought much about it, but we decided that we were enjoying the children, felt good about doing what God wanted us to do and healthy enough to keep having them. It was true that they would be an additional financial burden, but somehow God always came through with a big policy sale or a very good year for the agency. We had faith in Him and He didn't disappoint us."

Bill and Barbara took a break from business and child rearing to join a dance class at Philadelphia Country Club. "While we both felt that we were fairly good ballroom-type dancers, we admittedly knew nothing about the rumba, samba, tango, etc., and we were interested in learning about them." The group showed off the new steps at Thursday night buffet dinners at the club, where the $4.50 price plus tax and tip was considered a remarkably low price even in the 1950s.

Bill notes that a member of the dance group, Bob Bauman, whom he had tried unsuccessfully to recruit as an agent, eventually became chief executive officer of Smith Kline Beecham. Bill told him with a smile, "I guess you're better off where you are."

The children remember their father's love of dancing. He and daughter Tez often made a lively pair on the dance floor at family celebrations. "I would always try to lead," Tez said, "but he liked how tall I stood. I had too much hip action. He wanted me to be stiff like he was."

Minna has this memory: "I was coming home one night, and Dad had his music playing in the den next to their bedroom. Dad said, 'Minna, let's dance to this,' so we danced around the bedroom while Mom watched. Dad just loved dancing."

Bill and Barbara faced an addition to their financial burden when they decided to look for a larger house than the one in St. Davids. "We found a perfect house for us—10 bedrooms, well taken care of on two acres of ground on a quiet street in Haverford, also on the Main line. It was about an eighth of a mile from the hotel where we had our wedding reception and stayed with the 'chicken pox' children. The only snag at that moment was the asking price—$90,000."

A couple could obtain a 20-year mortgage from Equitable with interest of four and a quarter percent, but the maximum loan was two-thirds of the purchase price (up to $40,000). That meant offering only $60,000 for the home, and the sellers received an offer of $70,000.

Barbara was deeply disappointed because she had her heart set on living in that house. A few weeks later the higher offer fell through, and the couple's bid was accepted. Now they had to sell the St. Davids property before the closing date on the Haverford home in late February 1964. "The weeks went by without getting any real offers. Barbara and I discussed it at length and finally decided that we and the older children would make a novena (a devotion on nine successive days praying for special situations) at early Mass at the Villanova Chapel, where we were married. Finally on the seventh day of the novena, our realtor received a bona fide offer for what we were asking, and the papers were signed a few days later. We naturally finished the final two days of the novena with the realization that they really do work. All ended happily, and we lived in that wonderful house until 1986."

Paul ("Chet") was the first baby to arrive in the new house on November 9, 1964, followed by Andrew ("Buck") on January 5, 1967 and Alexandra ("Lexa"), the 15th of the Walsh children, on January 23, 1968.

Long hours at work, the growing family and the move to Haverford took a toll on Bill's golf, although he recorded several significant triumphs. He finally won the Plainfield club championship over his friend Frank O'Brien and added a second championship at Philadelphia Country Club. He again reached the finals of the New Jersey Better Ball Championship with O'Brien. The *New York Times* carried a photo of the four finalists on the front page of its sports section. Bill missed qualifying for the U.S. Amateur Championship by three strokes. His membership at Philadelphia Country Club restricted him to weekday play in the beginning, and when that limitation expired so he could play there on weekends, he attempted to convert to a non-resident membership at Plainfield, but the New Jersey club had no such membership, so he resigned (but not permanently).

The Walshes brought their well-used Studebaker from New Jersey to Philadelphia, then moved up to a new Plymouth and later a large Ford station wagon. Then came a Volkswagen bus for Barbara and a small Chevrolet for Bill, which he purchased from Roger Penske, a fellow Philadelphia Country Club member. Bill has stayed with a Chevy through the years, leasing from Roger's brother David. Roger went on to success as a driver and owner of racecars. He still carries insurance he bought from Bill early in their relationship.

CHAPTER 8

Swimmin' Walsh Women

B y the late 1950s and early 1960s, swimming was competing with golf for attention in the Walsh household as the older girls started to represent Philadelphia Country Club in interclub meets. Bill, feeling that he had the responsibility due to having several swimmers in the family, became the club's swimming chairman for a few years, and Barbara took on the job of getting the swimmers to practices and competitions.

"It all really started when we belonged to Plainfield [New Jersey] Country Club," Barbara recalled. "There was a nice pool there, and Stephanie took a few lessons and started to swim. So when we came down here, Philadelphia Country Club was in the process of building a new clubhouse in Gladwyne. No other country club in the area had a 50-meter, Olympic-sized pool, but PCC did. We would go to the pool daily all summer. I would take a playpen with me, put the one-year-old in it so the baby wouldn't crawl into the pool, and the rest of the children would swim all day."

Frank Keefe, a Villanova student at the time, was the PCC coach when Stephanie was in the 10-and-under age group, and he really encouraged the girls with extra practice time, tough workouts and attention. Mary Freeman Kelly, an Olympic swimmer, and her husband, John B. Kelly

Jr., an Olympic rower, were PCC members. Mary and Keefe felt that the older girls would do very well by adding winter swimming, so an invitation to join her prestigious Vesper Boat Club swim team was extended. Daily practices were held at the University of Pennsylvania in the winter and Kelly Pool in Fairmount Park in the summer, when an afternoon workout was also added. Vesper's women's team was a national championship contender each season and by far the best team in the east by the early 1960s. Olympian George Breen soon joined forces with Kelly, and he coached several of the younger Walshes. Their coaching styles were very different, but both got great results.

Stephanie remembers the adventures of commuting to practice at Penn: "We were very independent at a very young age. I recall taking the train down to 30th Street Station at age 10, and we would walk over to the pool at Franklin Field. These days you'd have to walk through some pretty rough areas, but back then there would be a group of us arriving from the various suburbs, and we'd meet at 30th Street and walk over together. Mom would give us each one dollar, exactly the round-trip fare for under age 12 on the Paoli Local." As their involvement became more intense and before the girls got their drivers' licenses, Barbara would occasionally drive them to 6 a.m. practices before school. Bill regularly drove them down to Penn on Saturday mornings, spending their practice time at his mid-city office getting in some quiet work time. Later, when Huddie was training for the Olympic Trials in 1972, Bill got permission from Villanova to have her train in their 25-yard pool in the early mornings before school, while Bill ran in circles around the pool, acting as lifeguard. Barbara's and Bill's patience and perseverance with the demands as parents of a large family of swimmers paid off handsomely as several of the girls eventually achieved national and world ranking.

Some of the younger Walshes worked out at the old Aquarium Pool near the Philadelphia Museum of Art. To avoid having to wait for the children in the damp-and-dingy parents' waiting room, Barbara would remain out in the car, sewing needlepoint Christmas ornaments and other items.

Barbara recalls driving to a meet in Northeast Philadelphia one Sunday morning, when the tie rod in her car broke and the wheels turned inward. She was "scared to death" but thankful that no one was hurt. Bill, always so busy with work, did not get to many of the local or top-level competitions, nor did he or Barbara travel to any national championship meets. However, the 1967 nationals took place locally at Kelly Pool in Philadelphia. Stephanie had excelled the year before, placing sixth in the country in the 100- and 200-meter butterfly events in Lincoln, Nebraska. The event in Philadelphia was a different story. "I really had a poor meet," she said. "I really wanted to do well because Dad was watching; he had paid for all of my swimming and I wanted him to be proud of me and to know that all of his support was worthwhile. I think I was nervous about having him there in the stands. Dad was supportive, nonetheless, despite the fact that my performance was not up to my own high expectations."

Bill strongly encouraged the children to compete in sports. "It was healthy, it showed what commitment was all about, doing your best, trying to exceed your own goals and better yourself," recalls Bridget. "There were days when we didn't want to get up early and then dive into the cold water and work out hard for two to three hours, but those who wanted to compete at the national level, of course, had to do that. Competition for Dad was as much about competing with yourself as against someone else. You didn't have to win. You had to have a good attitude, do your best and be a good sport. You needed to strive to improve yourself. I think all of us would agree that one of his primary goals for us was to develop strength of character, commitment and faith."

Bridget says that her parents' "level-headed approach to competition, rather than watching every practice and tracking all of our times, was different from many of the other parents." In fact, when Huddie broke the American record in the 400-meter individual medley at the 1974 National Championships in Concord, California, she called home to tell her parents the good news. Barbara's response: "Is that a good time?"

The Walsh boys also swam proficiently for Philadelphia Country Club, but they turned to golf and other sports as they got older. Michael even held the national 10-and-under age group record for the 50-meter backstroke for several years. After a few years off, he returned to the pool at St. Joe's Prep, again having success in the backstroke events.

Several of the Walsh girls elevated their swimming careers to remarkably high levels. Stephanie competed nationally and ranked in the top 20 in the world in butterfly events in the mid-1960s. She coached several age-group teams in Pennsylvania, Connecticut and Massachusetts and went on to become the head women's coach at Harvard, which was the first women's full-time swim coaching job in the country. Bridget also competed nationally and swam at American University.

Minna swam in local and Middle Atlantic events and won many medals but says she gave up serious swimming at 14 "because I was interested in boys." Monica also did some swimming in her early years but soon decided that it wasn't for her.

Title IX, which bans sex discrimination in schools, was passed too late to allow swimming scholarship opportunities for the older girls, but Tez, Huddie and Maura were all able to further advance their swimming careers and accomplishments thanks to this legislation.

Tez, an outstanding backstroker, swam for Drexel University's men's team when it had no women's team. She helped to start and then captained the women's team and earned a full scholarship for her remaining two years there. She once scored 49 points by herself in the Eastern Championships to place 20th among 41 teams. She has been inducted into Drexel's Athletic Hall of Fame.

Huddie started college at Cornell but took time off to concentrate on swimming after her freshman year and placed fifth in the Olympic Trials in the 400-meter individual medley and eighth in the 200-meter butterfly in 1976, just missing a spot on the team. She received a full scholarship to swim at the University of Florida and swam to All-American honors there. After graduating from college, she became the assistant women's coach and head coach of the masters swimming program at the University of Texas (Austin). It was here that she met her future husband, Kevin Murray.

Maura earned All-American recognition in the 500-yard freestyle and won three Pennsylvania state high school championships in that event while at Harriton High School. Maura attended the University of Southern California on a full scholarship, won the 500-yard freestyle national championship as a freshman and was All American all four years at USC.

Masters swimming, a program started in 1970 for adult swimmers, has become a big part of the Walsh sisters' continuing fitness routines. Seven of them have swum in National and World Masters championship events, won many awards and qualified for top 10 nationally. "We even had T-shirts made up with 'Swimmin' Walsh Women' emblazoned on them," said Stephanie. The sisters have also become involved in the program's volunteer organization and have routinely had Walsh get-togethers around the country at Masters swimming events. At the 1985 Nationals at Brown University, for example, newspapers in Boston and Providence headlined the accomplishments of Stephanie, Tez and Huddie with the title "Swimming Walsh Sisters Enjoy Poolside Reunions and Success."

This great love of swimming has been passed along to the next generation. Several of Barbara and Bill's grandchildren have become involved in competitive swimming, reaching top levels in club, high school and college programs. And Frank Keefe, that coach who started Stephanie on the competitive swim road back at Philadelphia Country Club so many years ago, ended up coaching her son Steve Johnson at Yale University. Steve placed second in the Eastern Intercollegiate Championships in the 200-yard freestyle his senior year and continues to swim in the Masters program.

Now at Walsh family reunions, there is always a Walsh Swim Meet on the schedule. It is usually made up of several assorted relays, where family members of different generations are spread among teams to make them competitive. "It's great fun," Stephanie notes, "and about 40 of the Walsh kids and grandkids participate. Mom and Dad are our biggest cheerleaders."

CHAPTER 9

Booth Lane Memories

The Walsh children experienced many colorful memories growing up in the house on Booth Lane in Haverford, with Christmas morning standing out in their minds. The strict discipline that pervaded their existence was very present as they eagerly anticipated the time to see their gifts. The large, mostly unfurnished living room served as the focal point.

Stephanie described the procedure: "The little kids would be up very early, of course, but they weren't allowed down the stairs. They had to wake up Mom and Dad, and then they'd have to wake up all of us, and then we'd have to get in line, youngest to oldest, and Dad would say, 'I want to see if Santa came.' The kids are waiting breathless and squealing at the top of the stairs, and Dad would go down and turn on a tape recorder—he never did movies—and turn on the lights on the two trees."

Finally they all got to enjoy their pile of gifts. "They didn't wrap anything," Bridget recalls, "because that would have been horrendous."

Later, the exchange of Pollyanna gifts lasted until dinnertime, according to Monica. "There was a point where everybody was giving gifts to everyone," she said, "so it would just take hours and hours. Then we'd have our big formal dinner. It was a whole day of just being with the family."

Business was not far from Bill's mind even on Christmas day. "One time Dad went out in the middle of the extravaganza," Stephanie noted, "and sold three life insurance policies to a Jewish family that wasn't celebrating Christmas. Nobody even missed him."

The family trimmed two Christmas trees every year—"Dad's Tree" and "Mom's Tree." Bill's tree in the living room featured homemade ornaments. "We all helped decorate," Huddie remembers, "but we dreaded the gleaming icicles Dad insisted on using on the big tree. Whenever we tried to just throw a bunch on, he'd catch us and make us redo it, one strand at a time." Barbara's tree stood as a greeting in the front hall with ornaments limited to gold, silver and blue. "That was a fun time being able to put up both of those trees," Maura said, "but Mom pretty much took care of hers because she wanted it to be perfect. The house was always really well decorated because Mom always had Dad's agency party before Christmas."

That mammoth unfurnished living room housed another popular activity for the kids. "Walsh sports did not end in the evening or in the winter," Tim explained. "We found a way to play most sports inside the house in our empty living room, which had six sets of French doors. Chipping and putting with real golf balls. Full-court basketball with the fireplace mantel on one end and the top of the door frame on the other. Wiffle ball. Running bases with a hardball or tennis ball. Floor hockey with street hockey sticks, tennis balls or homemade foil balls if my Dad had locked up all the tennis balls. We even made goalie pads from an old foam mattress. The goals were created by the space beneath a large rectangular table positioned at each end of the room. We even played tackle football in there sometimes.

"The room was big and obviously had lots of windows. It also had no curtains. We broke every window in there at least a few times. Some—at slap-shot level—were probably broken more than 10 times. Dad would get very angry with us, and it was a continual battle. We'd see the lights of his car turn into the driveway from the living room and all run for cover. He would usually see us as well. I think some of our worst spankings came from that. Some were by hand, some by umbrella—if it happened to be raining out. Times were different then, of course, but we never got hit unless we deserved it."

Maura remembers, "We didn't have lots of toys or cool stuff, but we made do with what we had. It must have been 1968 or 1972 during the Olympics when we younger kids were all so excited that we made our own Olympic games inside the house. We set up about eight different events in the living room, including the high jump where we did the Fosbury Flop over the couch into a large pile of pillows. We even had a marathon, running around the house, up and down the front and back stairs at least 20 times. Danny always won everything. He was the best athlete as a kid. Of course, Dad knew nothing of these events. If he had, we would have been in trouble. Mom just put up with it."

When Bill and Barbara went out at night, the games started. "We used to think how smart we were," Chet recalls. "Somebody was on watch to look for their headlights. We'd flick the lights off and run upstairs. They'd come in and make us line up. They saw the lights go off, and they could see everybody running upstairs."

The kids even managed to inject games into the burdensome chore of raking leaves on the sprawling Haverford lawn. "Yard work and sports often collided," according to Tim. "If we were out working in the yard, we would eventually find a ball somewhere and start playing something. In the fall, we usually had a football hidden in one of the leaf piles and just waited for my dad to leave or go inside. As soon as he did, we were playing three-on-three or two-on-two football. Sometimes all we could do was sneak in a few throws while my dad was around front or back. Dad caught on pretty quickly and started to confiscate any ball he came across. He locked them in a closet in the house or hid them other places. We eventually found the key and would pull them out one by one as needed.

"Unfortunately, we did not discriminate as to which balls we used. One time, we came across an interesting looking brown-and-white football that we had not seen before. It was very cool. We used it for a while before my dad realized it was missing. It turned out to be a ball commemorating Villanova's Liberty Bowl appearance in 1962. Needless to say we had worn it out pretty well.

"The worst was a baseball we used to play 'running bases' on our driveway. The ball was hidden away in this closet with the other balls my dad had confiscated, but it was on this little ball holder. It had some signatures on it that did not mean much to us at the time. The day we took it out was a little wet, and the driveway nicked the ball up pretty much. It turned out to be a ball autographed by Babe Ruth and Lou Gehrig, although there was no way to know that after we got done with it."

Bill was typically determined to make sure the leaf raking was meticulous—especially on Thanksgiving Day, when the family gathered for dinner. "Dad was adamant that there would be no leaves on the grass," Maura said. "He would work until the last hour when the guests would arrive. The yard had to be perfect, even though no one would be outside to see it. I think he was just trying to teach us to work toward a goal and achieve it. The best part of those raking marathons was the large leaf pile in the backyard next to the old garage. After we had dumped a number of large sacks in the pile and it was nice and fluffy, we would take turns jumping out of the second-floor window of the garage apartment into the pile. It made all the work worth it."

Tim also feels there was a lesson in Bill's insistence on doing things right: "He recognized good work loudly, criticized sloppy work and always made you redo something that was not done properly. I'm still not a big fan of yard work, but I can't ignore the tremendous feeling of accomplishment I get when I finish weeding my flower bed, raking my yard, shoveling snow, trimming my hedge, etc. I think we all have carried that strong work ethic with us into our adult lives."

Bill instilled that work ethic at an early age through a Sunday newspaper delivery route for the now-defunct *Philadelphia Bulletin*. Michael took over a neighbor's route that grew into the Walsh Boys News Service (later the

Walsh Boys and Girl News Service when Lexa joined the effort.) "Dad clearly had ideas that the boys at a young age should know what the responsibility of work is," Dan remembers. "So there we were at seven years old going out and delivering papers. It was a time for us to be together, a commitment to waking up early and doing habit-forming work. It was a way of letting the rope loose a little bit and seeing if we could do it on our own."

Bill said the Sunday morning schedule was very strict: "I'd wake each one going on the route at 6 a.m. If he didn't get right up, I'd be back five minutes later with a cold, wet washcloth. Anyone who was still not up after the next five minutes would get a glass full of cold water poured on him, although this didn't happen often."

The deliveries were planned down to the last detail. "Dad would drive us to strategically positioned spots and drop us with four or five Sunday papers, and we'd meet him at the next intersection," Tim said. "He had multiple boys dropped in different places and had all the logistics worked out."

With the delivery complete, the team went to 7:30 a.m. Mass at Our Mother of Good Counsel Church in Bryn Mawr and then home to breakfast cooked by Bill—two poached eggs on wheat toast. Often the eggs got overcooked, Minna pointed out, so the children called them "bullets."

The children then cleaned up the kitchen, and it was time to start on the chores Bill assigned for the day. If they completed the work by 3:30 in the afternoon, they were rewarded with golf at Philadelphia Country Club.

The Walsh News Service went out of business abruptly in 1982, when the *Bulletin* ceased publication, but there was a happy ending when a previously stingy customer gave the children a $500 tip. Bill used the largesse to treat the boys to a round of golf at Plainfield Country Club.

The children remember the ordeal of monthly allowance meetings when Bill would total up the golf, tennis and food they had signed for at Philadelphia Country Club and deduct the amount from their allowances.

"As you got older," Maura pointed out, "you realized, 'wow, I can sign my name and sign the Walsh number and be able to get a free lunch on the terrace or buy a hamburger.' Dad would have this incredible bill coming from the club from all of us spending money that we really shouldn't have been spending. This was a lesson about money and paying for our own things."

Tim recalls, "By the end of summer many of us had a debt so big that it would take us all fall, winter and spring to pay it down just in time for the next summer. My dad used those meetings to embarrass the abusers and commend the non-abusers." Arguments often developed over the signatures.

Tez noted, "The meetings were always gloomy."

CHAPTER 10

A Letter to the Children

*This is a slightly revised letter written by Bill Walsh
to the Walsh children on September 1, 1969*

Dear Children,
Events of the recent summer seem to indicate that a letter like this is in order, even very necessary.

Our Love – Though you may wonder sometimes when we are very upset with one or more of you, Mommy and I do deeply love each and every one of you. It is this love that makes us want you home at a reasonable time at night, want to know with whom you are, and want you to do your best at whatever you undertake.

As you know, each of you is a flesh-and-blood part of each of us, something which you and we can never change.

Discipline – There are two principal types of discipline, that imposed by someone else on us (such as laws and parents' rules) and that which we impose upon ourselves.

In short, any time you do anything which you don't actually have to do, and which is harder on you than if you didn't do it, it is, in effect, a practice of self-discipline. Naturally, the reverse is also true—not doing something when it would be easier to do it (smoking, etc.).

It is evident in all walks of life that the person with the greatest amount of self-discipline will, everything else being equal, generally be the most successful.

Because human beings are not perfect and never will be (until they reach heaven), discipline of the first type is absolutely necessary in a civilized society and will continue to be. As the family is the basic foundation of any society, discipline of the first type is also a "must" in the day-to-day life within a family. Each generation passes through a phase when such discipline is resented and seriously questioned. Occasionally, attempts are made to ignore the rules completely, only to have the offender eventually realize the error of his or her ways.

Discipline of the second type (self-imposed), because it is voluntary, is not so common but is actually much more important in the makeup of an individual. To self-disciplined people, the law-and-order discipline of the first type is easy to understand and to live by. Obedience to law and order, to rules and regulations comes naturally and willingly, rather than resentfully.

Religion – Both Mommy and I are Roman Catholics, and are happy to be. We are trying to bring up each of you to realize the lasting benefits which are realized from trying every minute of your lives to be a good Catholic. At some inconvenience, and at considerable expense, we have seen to it that each of you attends Catholic school, as we feel very strongly that you will grow to better understand your religion and become a better Catholic by attending Catholic schools.

This is also why we insist upon your attendance at Mass, not only on Sundays, holy days and First Fridays, but encourage your attendance at daily Mass, particularly during Lent. These habits learned during youth will be of lasting value when you yourselves become parents, nuns or priests.

Patriotism – It goes without question that we expect each of you to believe in the United States and that for which it stands. We know that you respect the flag and will never do anything to disgrace it. If any of you is fortunate enough to participate in the Olympics, I know you will realize even more completely the importance of patriotism.

Family Loyalty – In addition to patriotism (loyalty to your country), there is another type of loyalty to which we are put to the test much more frequently – family loyalty. Just as disloyal, unpatriotic citizens weaken a country, so do disloyal members of a family weaken the family.

Although there have been strong disagreements within our family, and there will, I am sure, be many more, it is most important that these disagreements, no matter how emotionally violent they are, be kept within the four walls of our home, to the exclusion of outsiders, friends and even close relatives.

In a family as large and as well-known as ours, even the most trivial dispute tends to be blown up out of proportion, and hence this family loyalty is even more imperative. Throughout history, a well-bred family of high character will always stick together, particularly in times of crisis. We expect ours to do the same, no matter what anyone's individual feelings may be at a given time. For centuries, the principle, "Do not hang out your family's soiled linen," has been handed down as one of the cardinal rules of family life.

Character – Though it is still popular to refer to a rather strange or different person as a "character," and each person God has ever created is in the strict sense a distinctive character, we mean something a little different here. To have the character meant here, we must at all times be:

Unscrupulously Honest – To have justifiably earned a reputation for always telling the truth, for playing a game according to its rules and never cheating in any activity is probably the greatest asset a person can have in dealing with his fellow man.

Striving to Improve Ourselves – Through reading, study, athletic activity and participation in various school, civic and charitable endeavors, we should continually attempt to better ourselves. It is impossible to stand still. We either go ahead every day or we go backward. If God has been so kind to give us certain abilities, we should take all reasonable and practical steps to become as proficient as possible in those sports or activities.

Unselfish – Unselfishness is an admirable quality in anyone, but in a large family it is imperative. Selfishness and self-centeredness cannot be tolerated under any circumstances.

Helping Others – Somewhat overlapping on unselfishness is helping others, but we do strongly adhere to the belief that we were put here by God to do more than merely satisfy our own whims and desires. When it comes our turn to die, let's hope that we can honestly say that we have contributed to our fellow man and that the world is a better place because we were here.

Participation in school, civic, club and charitable activities is simple, yet a very important and practical way of making a definite contribution to society.

What I'm trying to say more than anything else is that we don't want to see our children become selfishly wrapped up in themselves, so that because of laziness and/or indifference, they avoid important tasks which they are capable of performing. It is, unfortunately, a common cry of many people with very little to do, "I'm too busy" when asked to help with some civic or charitable work.

Practicing Good Sportsmanship – A family as interested in athletics and various competitive sports, etc. as ours will have exposure to many good sports and unfortunately a few poor ones. No one is less attractive at the time than a poor sport.

It is most important that we do our best at all times to win fairly, but no one wins all the time. When we do lose, we should do so gracefully, with a smile, a ready handshake and with our congratulations to those who beat us. Never do we want anyone to start giving excuses which in any way take away from the other person's victory or attempt to put the blame for our defeat on anyone or anything else ("I was sick." "I'm not used to such slow greens." "The pool wasn't lighted well enough" etc.). Take your defeat like a man, and resolve that next time you meet, you'll win.

I stress this point because I am convinced that more character is developed in athletics as a preparation for the hard knocks of life than in any other way.

Being Ladies and Gentlemen – We, of course, expect each of you to be polite and respectful to others at all times, and in particular to your teachers, priests, parents of your friends, our friends, in fact any older person, and to us. This embodies again a smile, a pleasant greeting and general all-around politeness and courtesy.

It also means that your language will at all times be that of which you know Mom and I would not disapprove. The use of crude, profane or abusive language is indicative of poor judgment, a poor vocabulary or a surly or "don't give a darn" attitude. Needless to say, any such language will not be tolerated.

There's an old saying that "one should always put his best foot forward." This means neatness and cleanliness in dress and overall appearance, a smile, a steady look in the eye and a vocabulary completely free of crudeness, profanity and surly remarks.

Common Sense – (smoking, drinking, driving, etc.) It goes without saying that anyone who takes up smoking today has to care very little about his wellbeing. Anyone even trying drugs has to have even less common sense. As you know, Mom and I are both moderate drinkers, and we believe that nothing is wrong with such moderation. However, we would expect that you would not drink away from home until you are of age to do so and have first learned at home how to drink.

Teenage auto accidents many times result in the death of one or more persons and occur so frequently that auto insurance rates have become prohibitive. It has been proven that these accidents do not occur because the teenagers are actually poor drivers but rather because they had been drinking, were going too fast for conditions or were showing off for their friends. In many cases, the cause of the accident is a combination of all three of these reasons.

Dating, Curfews – While this subject is vast enough to warrant an entire book, I merely want to summarize Mom's and my feelings on this subject.

We encourage you to have dates, preferably on a double or triple basis until you are engaged or close to it. We also encourage your dating many different people until you find the person whom you honestly believe you could be happy with for the rest of your life. Real love takes many more than a few dates, and should not be confused with physical attraction, which can happen with a mere look, a dance together, etc. Marriage is a continuous test of genuine love, and the primary reason for so many divorces is that the marriages were not founded on real love but rather on a physical attraction or infatuation.

We have imposed, and will continue to impose, a 12:30 a. m. curfew on all dates, unless a special situation occurs for which special permission must be obtained.

In the rare situations where permission has not been obtained and you find you will be later than 12:30, we insist that you telephone us.

Our reason for the curfew is simple—more wrong things happen late than early, more accidents, more temptation, etc. It is our accountable mission as parents to do our best to bring you to marriage or the religious life in the most eligible state. We know that a reasonable curfew will help us to do that.

Education –Though we hope that each of you wants to go to college, we realize that it is possible that some of the girls might want to go to business school, nursing school, art school, etc.

We hope that wherever possible, scholarships, in whole or part, may be won by some of you. Nevertheless, though the burden will be great on us, Mom and I will make every possible sacrifice to see to it that each of you who wishes will go to college (for an education, not to fool around).

SUMMARY – This has been a long letter, yet I hope it clarifies many of the more important points of our relationship with each other. We are a large family, an important family, and hopefully we shall remain a religious family as well as an intensely loyal and patriotic one.

We want your love, obedience and respect in return for our love, respect and fair and considerate understanding.

Mommy and I are not perfect; no human being is. We have made mistakes and will, I'm sure, make others. We have undertaken a tremendous responsibility in having, with God's help and inspiration, as many children as we have. Without such help from God and courage on our parts, some of you wouldn't be a part of this world. We did have each of you, however, because we deeply love each other and because we wanted to help God have more souls who would eventually unite with Him in heaven.

Furthermore, we believed that with our seeming good health, my education, the probability that I'd be able to provide the necessary financial resources and again with God's help, we'd be able to successfully raise all of you.

It's a tough struggle, but we still believe as we did many years ago. We just want you to also realize what goes on and to fully appreciate that our family is something special, deserving the loyalty and united effort of all of us.

Love,

Dad

CHAPTER 11

Bill Responds to 9-11

Bill Walsh wrote this letter on September 17, 2001.

Dear Walsh Family,

On this day, which also happens to be our 53rd wedding anniversary, I thought it a good idea to get off a letter to each of you concerning the tragically shocking events of last Tuesday, September 11.

Amazingly, as large as our family is, we were very blessed to have survived the past week with no personal losses or injuries. (Some of our friends were not as fortunate.) Dan and Lexa were both in Europe, but thanks to Buck, we learned that Dan's plane never left London, and Lexa notified us that she was OK—a great relief to all of us, as were the calls and e-mails from the rest of you.

A good feeling that came out of all the turmoil was the realization that each of our family members really cares about and loves one another—a wonderful reassurance for Mom and me.

As I told you in my long letter of September 1, 1969, we are a special family. While this is largely true because of our numbers, it is made even more specially so because of the love we have for each other.

Of particular note in recent days is the outpouring of public sentiments of loyalty to our country and of the desire to be close to God. And this was particularly evident in our local churches, where attendance yesterday was 30 to 50 percent higher than normal.

It showed that most people turn to God in times of crisis, and the catastrophes of last Tuesday certainly pose a serious crisis in our country. Life here will probably never be the same.

We hope and pray that all of you realize how much more easily you will be able to handle this and future tragedies if you are close to God. Mom and I could never have raised all of you without a very strong relationship with God and the firm belief that He would take care of all of us.

Now that each of you is an adult and on your own, and even though we will be praying for you and your children each day, we strongly believe that everything will be better if each of you is also close to God.

In doing this, the example you set for your children and your and their friends will be an extra benefit to them and to you. Also, you are then much more capable of handling the problems that you are certain to face. God never gives us a problem which, with His help, we cannot accept and solve.

Some of you may be asking a very legitimate question after last Tuesday's horrible events—how could God allow this to happen? While no one can answer this completely, it is because each human being is created with a free will, and sometimes humans do terrible things. Though God could have created us without such freedom, we would then be mere robot-like creatures and unable to experience all the joys of life here on earth.

So, the answer has to be—we have to live our lives as best we can, keep close to God, and trust in Him to help us live the lives He wants us to enjoy, so that we will someday be with Him in heaven.

We're not trying to "shove religion down your throats," as the saying goes, but we do sincerely believe that each of you will be able to handle life's problems better if you follow these suggestions. Some of you are already doing this; we hope the others will also.

We love each of you very much.

Mom and Dad

CHAPTER 12

Growing Up "Walsh"

The experience of growing up in the Walsh household depended somewhat on when you arrived. The younger children had the benefit of their elders' wisdom and support. And they enjoyed a relationship with a father whom they say had mellowed with age. They recall frustration with Bill's strict discipline and infrequent praise but look back today with respect and understanding. While their father was consumed with the insurance business and playing golf, they say unanimously that their mother was always there for them.

"A lot of times Dad was gone, and we sometimes resented that growing up," Bridget recalls. "He felt that it was important that he be the disciplinarian. If he was going to have a family of this many children, he needed to make sure that no one who might think of criticizing him would have reason to criticize him. He wanted to be above reproach. He wanted all of us to be above reproach. Of course, when you have a family of 15 children, that's pretty impossible. I think all of us looking back on how he functioned as a father with 15 children marvel at his ability to maintain his sanity with all the pressure of having to support us and support us very well."

Tim found his parents' contrasting approach an excellent blend: "I spent a lot of energy trying to earn my dad's respect—often at the expense of my mom. Her support was unwavering over the years for all the kids. I was so busy trying to get my dad's approval that I sort of took my mom's support and love for granted. Their parenting styles were very complementary. In hindsight, it was really a perfect parenting match. My dad criticized and pushed us to do more, to be better all the time. My mom encouraged us and supported us at every turn."

Michael shared similar feelings: "With a family like ours, Dad needed to be the tough guy, and my mom was the loving, compassionate one. It was definitely good cop-bad cop. We're all hard workers, and Dad taught us that. A lot of present-day parents could take some cues from him. We learned a lot from his gentlemanly nature in terms of competition."

Buck said of Barbara: "She was just a consistently graceful woman under so much pressure. You wonder how she managed to keep her cool with all the nagging and hassling she had from all of us over the years, the simple things like 'I don't want to eat my spinach.' I probably would have grabbed the spinach and stuffed it down my throat. The patience she had was remarkable."

From Dan's viewpoint as the 10th child born to Bill and Barbara, his mother served as "manager of the work force," while the older girls took care of the younger children. "The four older girls," he said, "had a sense of duty and work ethic that was just incredible. You still see it now. My aunt once said the girls are on a mission to get the job done. If you've ever seen any Walsh girls at a party, they're all caterers. They will take over. Some people would invite them to a party just to make sure the work gets done."

The younger children, Dan recalls, also had the Walsh work ethic but could enjoy life without the responsibilities faced by the older girls and Michael, the oldest boy. Buck, the 14th born, said, "The overall love and affection I received from the whole Walsh clan was amazing."

Bridget's siblings echo her belief that Bill was a man of "incredible integrity and incredibly high standards" with high expectations for them. Tim noted, "My dad was always a tough critic and not much for false praise or trying to encourage you. He was usually toughest when we succeeded at something and the most lenient and encouraging when we lost. He reminded us often not to get a big head, be a braggart or get too comfortable—something we all took to heart. As I got older, I sometimes resented the perceived lack of support and the criticism. I sort of took an 'I'll show you' attitude. It was a good, if not entirely positive, motivator for me. To this day, I still expend an inordinate amount of energy seeking my dad's approval."

Maura was proud to place second in three events at the Eastern Regional Swimming Championships when she was 14 or 15, but Bill suggested she could have placed first if she had worked harder. "He really pushed us," she said. "The attitude he had with all of us was we could always be better if we put in more work or did something else. And he did it, so he was a great example to prove that it was true. My feeling about Dad's prodding was 'I'm going to prove to him that I can do it my way.' When I got my scholarship to USC, that was the first time he ever told me he was proud of me."

Chet became a truly outstanding golfer with Bill's help, but he was not immune from criticism on the golf course. He once needed to get down in two putts from about 20 feet to win a hole from Bill in a club match. He ran the first putt several feet past the hole and faced a challenging second putt, which he made. But Chet heard no words of praise for winning the hole: "He lectured me walking to the next tee about how stupid I was going for it with the first putt when I needed to learn to be conservative and take the sure thing."

However, Buck concludes this about Bill: "As time has passed, I learned that he was always our fiercest critic to our faces but was in fact very supportive of us behind our backs." And from Bridget: "He never expected more of us than he expected of himself." Said Brendan, "He took pride in everything he did, whether it was for doing work in the yard, in his career or on the golf course. He always had a terrific attitude. He was a great role model. I never saw the day where he hadn't shaved or didn't have his shirt tucked in. He was always leading by example. Everyone looked up to him. He was a doer and a giver. He respected people no matter who they were, what they did or where they came from.

These are all traits that I practice in my life and have passed along to my own children as well as my staff."

Minna feels fortunate to work closely with her father today in the insurance business. "Dad's such a different person than he was while I was growing up," she finds. "He was so strict. He was very bossy, but then he was a boss in his work life. Mom was nurturing and not very strict, and Dad was the strict one. But sometime in the early '70s when Dad read the book *'I'm OK – you're OK'* (by Thomas A. Harris), apparently he changed his outlook on being strict. He definitely changed his attitude toward the kids after he read that book."

Lexa marvels that her "nice, Catholic, conservative parents who created this zoo" managed to keep things under control during the hectic years of the 1960s and '70s. "They kept a balance," she said, "of always letting us know what their concerns and values were while letting us have free will and be the people that we were."

Certainly this era challenged both parents and children. Dan credits the older girls who came of age in the '60s for "hacking out the ground in which the younger boys got to reap the benefits of a softer, gentler set of parents." Today, he says of Bill and Barbara, "They are so gentle, they have such faith, they are not closed to anything, they are open to everybody and different faiths. They have so expanded their vision of the world and what a person could be and how they can be happy because they saw all these different kids grow up and turn into normal, loving, good people under their guidance. I do believe that we were bigger because of our parents, but the kids made them bigger, too, more expansive through what we exposed them to. It was a two-way street."

Michael recalls, "We did have our differences when I was a teenager. I had the long hair and went through my hippie phase a little bit, so there were definitely some generation-gap issues, but we weathered the storm pretty well."

And from Barbara's point of view, there were some stormy days in the '60s: "It was such a difference from what we expected. We thought some of our kids would be nuns and priests. When I was young, I never went up against my parents. I don't remember ever talking back to them. I never did anything they didn't want me to do."

Tim Walsh summarizes his parents' virtues:

–The biggest thing I've observed over time about both my mom and my dad is their consistency and conviction in what they believe.

–They were always clear about their values, but they never preached them.

–They held true to their values—regardless of others' criticisms and doubts or their own tough circumstances.

–They let their actions speak for them more than their words.

–It was never just about them. They were never more important than the situation around them.

–They demonstrated tremendous respect for others in every situation. They were generous with their words, their time, their good wishes and their possessions.

–My dad, in particular, was extremely disciplined.

–They had a tremendous work ethic—something I think every kid has taken forward.

–They showed unwavering courage, honesty and trust.

The thing that's left a big mark on me about my parents is the power of these things over time. There is not a lot of immediate gratification in these traits. It's the confidence and conviction you gain on your own by being true to your values and having the courage to stick with them over time. I think that's the real gain in life. It may be the most valuable, but it's also the hardest to see along the way. I see my parents as models of that.

Bill's emphasis on discipline earned him the nickname "Sarge," first bestowed by Buck and picked up by other children. Buck remembers, "He'd say, 'Come on, rake the leaves, gash sakes, you kids haven't raked the leaves over there, you missed this.'—that kind of regimental approach to the chores we were responsible for doing."

"Gash sakes" was as profane as Bill got. "I don't know that Dad ever cursed," Tez said. " 'Gash sakes' was his curse whenever he was disappointed in us." Added Stephanie, "We heard that our whole lives."

Among the children's memories of Bill compiled for his 75th birthday:

"You don't often show your 'soft' side, but one of your weaknesses is new babies. We always loved, and still tell people about, the ritual we had of all sitting around Mom's and your bed when you arrived home with the newest addition while you stood proudly in the doorway. We each got a chance to hold the new baby and officially welcome him or her into the family. To this day, whenever a new grandchild arrives, we notice you sneaking a good look into their little faces and a gentle caress around the backs of their necks, just like you did with us."

CHAPTER 13

Barbara's "the Glue"

Several of the Walsh children cautioned the author during interviews not to overlook their mother's exceptional qualities and her importance as the family developed so admirably. Bridget summarizes their most common description of Barbara: "Mom is very important in the picture of our family because she's the glue that holds us together." The children frequently mention her incredible grace under pressure.

Says Brendan: "My mother is really a very special person. Her patience is unbelievable when you think about as teenagers how we treated her from time to time. I remember in high school if my mother was 10 minutes late to take me to basketball practice or to meet the bus for the game how I would chew her out, and she never lost her cool. It was just unbelievable what she was able to accomplish each and every day. She taught us a sense of compassion and respect for people and just to be kind. She cares about people. Anytime you wanted to bring someone over or have a sleepover, no problem. She rarely said no. One more person didn't upset her.

"She is one of the most compassionate people that I know, one of the most generous people that I know, and caring and loving, and we all get that from her."

Lexa agrees: "She's just the kindest, most graceful person ever. When

I was a kid, I was difficult for her, and I didn't mean to be. I think it was a matter of wanting more of her attention and being a pain-in-the-butt kid." Lexa recalls a time during college when, never reluctant to be different, she colored her hair purple, and Barbara walked through Suburban Square hand-in-hand, arm-in-arm with her. "She just didn't care what anybody thought," Lexa says, "and I thought that was really big of her. I didn't look like she wanted me to look, but she just embraced that this is who I am. She's just been incredibly supportive of my decisions."

Barbara remembers the purple-hair experience: "We were walking down the street in conservative Main Line Ardmore, and I thought, 'This is my daughter, and I love her,' so I just put my arm around her and walked with her. I thought, 'This is the way it's going to be. I'm not going to be ashamed of her. I don't like how it is but she's ours and we love her.' "

Today, Barbara says of Lexa, "She's wonderful. She's fun. We're very close. My proudest moment is my children."

Matt notes that Barbara always wanted to make sure every child checked in after being out at night: "My poor mom spent every night waiting until every kid was home before she went to sleep, which is pretty amazing." Somehow, he says, his mother found time away from child-raising to work frequently as a volunteer in numerous school and club activities.

Tim appreciates Barbara's way of handling people who were disagreeable by "killing them with kindness."

Comments Maura: "She was always there to support you in all things. If you didn't do well, she always told you that you did fine. She never put you down."

One more fond memory of Barbara from Chet: "If we ever wanted anything, we went to our mom because if we went to our dad, we knew the answer was going to be no. We had a chance with my mother."

CHAPTER 14

Eagles, Warriors and Wildcats

Although Bill was often too busy to spend time with the growing children, he did treat them to tickets to games in Philadelphia and at Villanova. The children still rave about those experiences.

Michael recalls some of the highlights:

"I have lots of fond memories of my childhood related to sports and sporting events, which sometimes included spending quality time with Dad. I remember getting the nod to go to the Eagles football games on home Sundays, especially 1960, a successful year when they advanced all the way to the NFL Championship game. I was lucky enough to join Dad for the big game. We took the train to 30th Street Station and walked all the way to Franklin Field, a long trek for a wee six-year-old, but it was pure joy, and what a great game it was as the Eagles hung on to defeat the Green Bay Packers. I'll never forget that image of Chuck Bednarik holding down Jim Taylor in the waning seconds of the game. Dad would take us as children to the PGA event at Whitemarsh Valley Country Club, which was very exciting as I got to see Ben Hogan and Sam Snead play, as well as the stars of the time, Jack, Arnold, Lee Trevino and others.

"We went to see the Philadelphia Warriors with Wilt Chamberlain play Cincinnati with Oscar Robertson at the old Convention Center. Dave

Zinkoff was at the mike that night, and somehow I ended up winning a salami. It was a big night for me, and Dad was thrilled.

"I also remember lots of trips to the Penn Palestra to see our beloved Villanova Wildcats in their Big Five matchups—lots of exciting, close games and great memories of that building. On one such night, after a few too many hot dogs and Cokes on the way home, I lost my lunch all over Dad—not a pretty sight. 'Gash sakes' was as close to cursing as he would ever get, but it showed he meant business, and I felt pretty badly about it. All was forgiven, and it was the last time I drank a Coke at a sporting event."

Trips to see the Eagles also bring special memories to Brendan: "To be able to spend an afternoon with our father was always something you looked forward to."

Tim emphasized that Bill "carved out quality time" for the children from his busy schedule. The boys started as young as age nine to take the train to meet Bill at the Palestra for Villanova games. "It was a good confidence builder for city living later in life for me," Tim said. He also looks back on 50-cent sky-deck tickets for Phillies games at Veterans Stadium "where you couldn't see the left fielder or center fielder if you sat in left field."

Monica has fond memories of Villanova basketball and football games: "It was something I loved to do with my dad. We didn't get much time with him because he was gone so much at work and everything, so to have that time was just really fun. I was a tomboy. I was really into sports, and I played football with my brothers, so it was a great time for me."

Said Maura: "I remember going to the Villanova basketball games at the Palestra and being so excited about it. This was during those years when Villanova made it to the finals of the NCAA. Those were really exciting times for the whole family, and I just remember thinking that I couldn't wait until my next turn to go."

"Dad's way of showing us that he loved us," Bridget noted, "was not the traditional hugs and kisses. It was like, 'I have tickets to the Villanova game.' I remember those clear, crisp autumn Saturdays going to the field for the football games."

In 1997, the Walsh children compiled 75 memories for Bill's 75th birthday. This memory focused on Villanova sports:

"We want to thank you for introducing us to Villanova University. We don't know what our family would have been like without Nova to cheer for. It reminds us of all the times we went to Retreat with you, and it always fell during the NCAA tournament or their conference tournament, and it always seemed like Villanova played on Friday night of Retreat. The rules of Retreat are that you have no connection to the outside world, and the good Catholic that you are, Dad, we know you would never break that rule. Wrong! Every year we would pile into your room and watch the Nova game on a small black-and-white TV that you would sneak into the room. We would have the sound down very low as we were not allowed to make a sound for fear of getting caught. You would even block the bottom of your door with a towel so the screen reflection wouldn't show through the crack. Safe to say, we were never caught."

CHAPTER 15

Meet the Children

Introducing the Walsh children in descending order of age:

STEPHANIE WALSH BEILMAN

As the oldest, Stephanie is the leader of the children, according to Bill, who says she is "understandably slightly bossy and a go-getter." Stephanie feels older children in a family are more likely to want to be like their parents than younger children, and she is a perfect example. Like Bill, she has been an outstanding achiever in education, business, sports and community service.

Stephanie attended high school at Holy Child in Rosemont, close to home, and began swimming year-round at the Vesper Boat Club in Philadelphia at age 10. While still a teenager, she ranked eighth in the world in the butterfly. She went to Marymount College in Arlington, Virginia, and continued swimming at the Northern Virginia Aquatic Club. She and her high school sweetheart, Tom Johnson, also a top swimmer, wed the summer after her freshman year and had two sons, Christopher and Stephen, before they divorced in 1976. Stephanie then resumed her education at Boston University and graduated magna cum laude in 1979.

Meanwhile, swimming remained an important part of Stephanie's life, not only as a competitor, winning many National Masters Championships, but as a YMCA coach in Pennsylvania and Connecticut. This experience led to her appointment as women's swimming coach at Harvard University, where she served from 1975 to 1980 until a letter from a recruiter paved the way for a career change to her father's business—insurance. The letter came from New York Life, but Stephanie wound up, like Bill, with Equitable Life, starting in 1980 at the company's office in Wellesley, Massachusetts. In 1984, she returned to Philadelphia as Bill's partner in Walsh Associates, where she works today.

Stephanie has gone on to serve as president of the Philadelphia Association of Life Underwriters, as a member of the Board of Directors of the Pennsylvania Association of Life Underwriters and as chairperson of the Host Committee for the 1996 national convention of the National Association of Life Underwriters. She is a Silver Knight of the Million Dollar Round Table. She has earned the designations of Chartered Life Underwriter, Chartered Financial Consultant and Chartered Advisor in Senior Living. She became the first female member of the Paoli-Malvern-Berwyn Rotary Club, where she was the first female president.

Stephanie was married again in 1997 to Donald Beilman, who has five children of his own. They live in Valley Forge. Her son Christopher, his wife Maggie and three children live in Berwyn. He works in sales for Dun and Bradstreet. Her son Stephen, his wife Penny and their two children live in West Chester, Pennsylvania. He works at Investor Force Inc. in Conshohocken.

In her spare time, Stephanie is president of the Colonials 1776 Masters Swim Team and head of the Valley Forge Cursillo Movement of the Philadelphia Archdiocese. She is very active in alumni activities at Holy Child, her high school, and St. Katharine of Siena, where she attended elementary school, and the Vesper Boat Club.

PAMELA JANE WALSH ("MINNA")

Minna has served as the office manager for Walsh Associates since 2002. Bill describes her as "very reliable, very competent, extremely conscientious and a great asset to us." She provided invaluable assistance in the production of the Walsh family story.

Although Minna was an honors student at Holy Child in Rosemont and posted high SAT scores, she recalls "working really hard, spending three or four hours a day on homework," so college did not hold much appeal for her. "We finally talked her into going to Villanova for a semester," Bill said, "but she didn't like it."

Minna recalls, "I didn't ever want much education. Back when I was 12, I wanted to be a mother of 22 kids because Mom had 12 kids at the time, and I wanted to be like Mom, only with more kids. And then I thought I might want to be an architect, but I didn't want to have to go to four years of college for that." She did take art classes and enjoys doing calligraphy and other artistic projects.

Before joining Walsh Associates, Minna spent 29 years as the office manager for open-heart surgeons in the Philadelphia area.

At age 17, Minna gave birth to a son, Pat, but gave him up for adoption since she could not support him. Two years later she married the baby's father, John Dowling. They lived in South Bend, Indiana while John attended Notre Dame, moved briefly to San Diego, and separated after they returned to the Philadelphia area. Although divorced, they remain friends.

Family members frequently laugh about John's introduction of a friend to Bill and Barbara: "I'd like you to meet Mrs. Walsh, affectionately known as Mommy Barbara, and this is Mr. Walsh, affectionately known as Mr. Walsh."

Minna met her son when he was 30 years old. She noted, "We've gotten to be very close. He's a radiation oncologist in Wilmington, North Carolina. He and his wife have two kids, and I usually go down to visit them a couple of times a year. He's gotten to meet his father, he met his father's parents before they died, and he's gotten to meet all of our family, so it's been great."

Minna and Steve Wood, who have been partners since 1983, live in Wayne, Pennsylvania, near Steve's two daughters and three grandchildren.

Like several of her sisters, Minna was an accomplished swimmer. Today she has many interests: "I really enjoy baking & cooking. I love to garden. I enjoy doing pottery and other types of crafts. I love music. I sing and play guitar. I get a lot of satisfaction from taking care of kids.

I babysit for my two grandchildren and for Steve's grandchildren. And I used to babysit a lot for our family, the doctor's family, and the neighbors. I guess you could say I'm definitely a motherly type."

BRIDGET KATHLEEN WALSH

Bridget started out on a familiar path for the Walsh girls: attending Holy Child and competing quite successfully in local and national swimming championships. She completed two years at American University, posting swimming records that lasted long beyond her stay there.

She interrupted her studies to pursue an interest in travel but returned to Philadelphia briefly, and while working at a restaurant in King of Prussia, she met her future husband, Criswell Davis, who had attended Episcopal Academy. They have been together since 1974.

Criswell had gone to college in Colorado, and when his hotel and restaurant work took them back to the mountains, Bridget studied art and textile design at Colorado State University.

She worked in several fields, most recently as a librarian in Kettering, Ohio, where they now live, and she spent time at home with their children, Cole, a graduate of Miami University of Ohio, and Teagan, a graduate of Columbia College in Chicago. Before college, they received home schooling from Bridget.

Bridget and Criswell were together for some time before they married. Criswell recalls Bill Walsh's somewhat hesitant acceptance of their relationship:

"We were back in Philadelphia for Christmas time in the big house on Booth Lane. The house was really busy, and I found myself in the kitchen with Mr. Walsh. It was an awkward moment. I said, 'Good morning, Mr. Walsh,' and he said, 'Good morning, Criswell.' After a brief amount of small talk, he looked at me and asked, 'Criswell, are you going to marry my daughter?' It wasn't an accusatory tone; it was just a very pragmatic question. I said, 'Mr Walsh, you're going to have to ask her.' He said, 'What do you mean?' and I said, 'Well, I've asked her every year for five years to marry me.' And his question was, 'Well, what does she say?' And I said, 'She asks me to ask her next year.' And he said, 'And you do?' I said, 'Yes,

I ask her every year.' And he thought about it for a moment, and he just looked at me and extended his hand, and he said, 'You can call me Bill.' He shook my hand, and I called him Bill from that point forward.

"It was a really touching moment where he just understood his daughter could be happy, and as long as she was encouraging me to ask her every year and I'm continuing to ask, he was OK with that. From then on my relationship with him just grew to be really close, and I consider him to be one of the most amazing men I've ever known in my life."

MONICA WALSH

Monica, a graduate of Harriton High School, has lived in California for many years. Since 1985, she has been active as a doula, which she describes as "a woman who supports and cares for new mothers and babies and their families in the first few weeks and sometimes months after their birth." She even continued to help one child for 10 years.

"He challenged me to my limit," Monica said, "and I realize that the reason that happened is that he reminded me of myself and how rebellious I was, so I know how challenging it was for my mom to handle me. I don't live inside the box. I live more on the edge. I follow my own spiritual path that is probably very different from anyone else in the family."

Monica also has completed the training to serve as a facilitator in Cellular Memory Release (CMR), an emotional release/healing technique that transforms old painful experiences and patterns from childhood so that an individual can move on to a more fulfilling life. It is a body-based technique that is much more efficient than talk therapy. Monica assists with CMR workshops and promotion.

A part-time caterer, she remembers producing dinner concerts in San Diego: "I would bring in traveling national folk musicians and Celtic musicians from Scotland and have about 200 people for dinner before the show. I loved it, but it was so much work. It was very rewarding, as I got to turn people on to lots of new music."

The many individuals whom Monica has served through her varied activities would agree with her assessment: "I am satisfied that I have made a huge difference in the lives of the people I've touched."

Her father said, "Monica has been a loyal, dedicated nurse to Barbara during her multiple surgeries. She seems very happy in California. We regret that we don't see more of her, but she has many good friends there."

MICHAEL JOSEPH WALSH

"Mike, as the first boy, received a lot of attention around the Walsh home but seemed to survive it all," his father pointed out.

Taking after his sisters, he became very active in swimming, and he held the U.S. Age 10 & Under backstroke record. Then, probably because most of his classmates were interested in basketball, Michael decided to give up swimming and take up basketball. "It was an understandable move," Bill said, "but being about five foot, five inches at the time, not a particularly good shot and not very quick, his basketball career didn't last long. He then concentrated on golf." It was a good choice, because Michael became an outstanding golfer.

At St. Joseph's Prep in Philadelphia, where he went to high school, he played on the golf team that won the Catholic League championship with teammates including Chris Lange, Jeff Kiley, Jim and John Finegan. Michael defeated his father in the semifinals of the Philadelphia Country Club championship and twice finished runner-up in that event. He reached the semifinals of the Golf Association of Philadelphia (GAP) Junior Championship and led the Pennsylvania Junior Championship for three rounds. He and his father won the GAP Father and Son Championship twice. He and Helen Sigel Wilson, one of the greatest women players in Philadelphia history, won the Women's Golf Association of Philadelphia Boyle Cup.

Michael went to the University of Florida with two other leading amateurs, high school classmate Lange and Chip Lutz, both of whom later enjoyed many years of success in GAP competition. The Florida golf team featured players such as Andy Bean, Andy North and Gary Koch, who became winners on the PGA Tour, so it was hard to break into the lineup. Michael did not play in matches against other colleges but did shoot 69 once to beat Bean in a practice round.

He interrupted college for a year to backpack around Europe, then earned a business degree at Villanova, lived in the Boston area briefly and relocated to Colorado Springs, where he managed a restaurant and, significantly, was exposed to the wine business. He then spent about a year in California, frequently visiting the Napa Valley wine country.

Michael moved back to Philadelphia in 1984 and soon began to work for a wine company. "I kind of rode the wave," he recalls. "I think my timing was excellent to get into the business just as wine was becoming a lot more popular and people were curious."

Michael has been with Majestic Wines and Spirits of Wayne, Pennsylvania, since 1990. He has taught wine classes at the University of Pennsylvania Wharton School and the Learning Annex, and he currently teaches at the Innkeeper's Kitchen, part of the Dilworthtown Inn in Chester County, Pennsylvania. He also gives private lectures for corporations and charities and travels around the world for business. "As much as I love selling wine," Michael noted, "my real passion is teaching about it."

He has never lost his passion for golf, but his work commitments keep him from the course. He belongs to the Pine Valley Golf Club and hopes to find more time for golf.

Divorced from his first wife, Michael became engaged on Christmas Day, 2010, to Hallie Boyce, a landscape architect from Baltimore. They were married in October, 2011.

THERESE WALSH SEIBERLICH ("TEZ")

Tez claimed a place in the ranks of outstanding swimmers among the Walsh girls, specializing in the backstroke. She started high school at Holy Child, transferred to Harriton High School and decided to attend Drexel University in Philadelphia, even though there was no women's swim team. That didn't faze Tez, who made the men's varsity team and won some backstroke races before becoming captain of the women's team when it resumed competition after cancellation during World War II. She became the second woman inducted into the Drexel Athletic Hall of Fame and went on to hold leadership positions with various aquatic organizations.

"Tez became our only daughter to take a strong interest in golf," according to her father, "and she successfully played on the Philadelphia Country Club women's team for many years." She belonged to the club for 24 years and became the first woman to serve on the Board of Governors. She and Bill placed second in the Griscom Cup, a Women's Golf Association of Philadelphia competition for golfers of opposite sex and different generations in the same family, the same year Matthew Walsh and his mother placed third.

She served as the volunteer general chairman of the 2003 United States Golf Association Women's Amateur Championship, which took place at Philadelphia Country Club. That position led to her employment as championship coordinator for Merion Golf Club when it held the 2005 U.S. Amateur Championship. She considered it a terrific compliment when people referred to Bill as "Tez Seiberlich's father" when she was usually "Bill Walsh's daughter."

Tez also served as assistant to the director of the McDonald's LPGA Championship, a major women's professional event.

She spent several years at Walsh Associates and held sales and management positions at other companies in Pennsylvania. In recent years she has been an active volunteer leader, including positions as chairman of the Audubon YMCA Advisory Board, co-president of the Woodland Elementary Home and School Association and treasurer of the Phoenixville YMCA swim team Parents Aquatic Club. She followed Bill and Stephanie as a Rotarian, belonging to the Havertown Club. Most recently she has been working in member relations and corporate sales for the Freedom Valley YMCA at Phoenixville. She frequently volunteers as a swim official for the YMCA and USA Swimming.

Tez has been married since 1993 to Bill Seiberlich, who is manager of communications for Saint-Gobain, a leader in the habitat and construction markets. They have two daughters in the Methacton School District in suburban Philadelphia, Meredith, an honors student involved in theatric productions, and Emma, another outstanding swimmer in the Walsh family.

HILARY WALSH MURRAY ("HUDDIE")

Michael Walsh at age two called his younger sister Hilary "Hud-di-die," which became "Huddie" or "Hud," as the family likes to call her.

Huddie followed the Catholic school-swimming pattern her sisters had established. "She always dressed as a nun on Halloween," her father said, "and we were sure she would become a nun." Huddie knew her parents' career preference: "I really think my dad had hoped I would become a nun, but I took the same route he did. I had lots of kids [seven] instead. I feel my parents and I have a special bond created primarily by the fact that I was one of the few kids who remained tied to the church through thick and thin."

After graduating from the School of the Holy Child, Huddie attended Cornell University for a year before taking time off to concentrate on swimming. She placed fifth in the 400-meter individual medley and eighth in the 200-meter butterfly at the 1976 Olympic Trials. "At that point," she noted, "Title IX had come into play, and several schools had money to offer for women's sports. It changed my life." Title IX is a law that requires athletic departments to offer programs in proportion to their gender population. Huddie received a swimming scholarship to the University of Florida and later moved to Austin, Texas to train with Paul Bergen, a highly regarded swimming coach at the University of Texas, where she became assistant coach of the women's swimming team under Bergen and eventually under the late Richard Quick.

Huddie earned a degree from Texas in elementary education and became a teacher. She met her future husband, Kevin Murray, while coaching an adult swimming program at the university, and they were married in 1984. "I thought I'd be here for only one year and then get the heck out of Texas," she recalls, "but now it's been over 30 years." During a relationship in Florida, Huddie gave birth to Meghen, now in her 30s, married and a mom, too. She and Kevin parented six children: Julia, Peter, Lesley, Kate, Tim and Dan, all at varying stages of young adulthood now.

Today Huddie feels fortunate to be nanny for her grandchild. Never far from a pool, she coaches a summer swimming league team, gives swimming lessons and volunteers at church, school and with swimming causes.

MATTHEW RICHARD WALSH

Matt did not find swimming as enjoyable as many of his siblings, but he performed well in basketball, baseball and golf. He attended Catholic schools into ninth grade before transferring to Harriton High School so he could play varsity basketball. He became one of the team's stars. Earlier Matt showed so much promise as a baseball pitcher that another player's father told Bill he had a chance to make the major leagues.

Following high school, Matt went to Juniata College intending to play basketball. After breaking his arm in a motorcycle accident, he completed his college education at Villanova, majoring in finance and playing on the golf team for one year.

Matt is an accomplished golfer who has belonged to Philadelphia Country Club since 1979. He and his father won Golf Association of Philadelphia Father and Son Championships in 1972 at Waynesborough Country Club and in 1980 at Brookside Country Club-Pottstown. Matt provided clutch birdies on the final hole of both alternate-shot tournaments, pleasing his father by reaching the green at the par-4 18th hole at Brookside with his drive.

He worked in insurance for an agency other than Walsh Associates for four years to experience the business from a different perspective, then joined Bill and Stephanie with Equitable in 1984. Today the three are individual sole proprietors in an office on Old Eagle School Road in Wayne, Pennsylvania, with Minna as office manager.

Matt, who has belonged to Ardmore Rotary with his father since 1985, became the club's youngest president. He has served on the Board of Directors of the Philadelphia Estate Planning Council and the Main Line Branch of the Red Cross.

Matt married his childhood sweetheart, Cristine, in 1984. They live in Berwyn near the office with their sons, Matthew Jr. and Greg, both graduates of the Villanova School of Business. Matthew Jr. is serving as an officer in the Marine Corps.

Spending time with his sons and their activities occupied much of Matt's attention away from the office: "The fact that they were close in age meant that they did a lot of things together. They played on baseball teams together, they played on football teams together, and they both wrestled from the time they were young. They used to have tournaments every weekend from December to March, and they even wrestled beyond that, depending on whether they qualified for other events. That was very time-consuming, so in a sense that's why I didn't have many hobbies. I was spending time with my kids, and it was well worth it."

TIMOTHY CHRISTOPHER WALSH

Tim has established his own marketing, communications and content development business in Massachusetts. He previously served as director of corporate marketing and director of corporate communications for technology companies.

Two family experiences years apart were noteworthy for Tim. After playing football, basketball and golf at Haverford School and attending Boston University for a year, he had saved enough money to take time off and live on the beach in Hawaii. He hitchhiked across the country and flew to Hawaii, ending up close to the Grand Wailea resort. Soon after he arrived there, his parents coincidentally came to the resort for a trip Bill and some of his agents had won.

"I spent the whole week with them when I wasn't working and had a great time," Tim recalls. "I was really impressed with how much respect the young guys working for my dad had for him. I think at that time I started to understand that my dad was a big role model for me. He lived his life the way he thought was right without being affected by what others around him thought or said. I was really proud of him and really proud to be his son."

Tim returned from Hawaii to graduate from the Boston University School of Public Communication. Fast forward to 1995, when Tim, Bill and five of the Walsh sons traveled to Ireland for a golf trip and to 1997, when all seven sons treated Bill to another journey to the links in Ireland. "On both trips," Tim noted, "my dad and I stayed on for a few extra days after everyone else went home to play a few more courses. I had organized both trips, and I think my dad was truly flabbergasted that I could put it all together. It was really bonding and spiritual for me. Between the land, the golf courses, the people there and the complete joy and sense of fulfillment I sensed in my dad, it just couldn't have been better."

Today Bill says of the trips, "Everyone in the family who was involved is most grateful to Tim."

Tim and his wife, Anna, live in Westford, Massachusetts with their children, Chloe, Anna's daughter by a previous marriage, and Colin.

DANIEL PATRICK WALSH

Bill is proud that Dan is a highly successful, internationally recognized artist, but he wasn't always thrilled with his son's career direction. "Danny," Bill once told him, "you're a great athlete and the hardest worker. I can't believe you want to be an artist and go to art school."

Bill recalls Dan's youth: "Dan was probably our best natural athlete. He aggressively participated in just about all sports. He was always one of the first players selected in any pick-up game. He also played good golf, caddieing at Merion and winning the caddie championship there. Somewhere along the line, he started to become interested in art. Barbara's sister Kathy was an artist of note, and probably that's how the genes reached Danny."

Dan actually studied forestry management for two years at New England College before transferring to the Philadelphia College of Art for his undergraduate degree and earning a master's degree in art from Hunter College of the City University of New York. While painting on the side, he developed a successful business as an electrical contractor in New York. Dan said of his father, "Once I was on my own two feet, he didn't care if I was an artist or an electrical engineer or a physicist as long as I could take care of myself."

After what Dan calls a "slow transition" from electrician to artist, galleries now represent his work throughout the United States and Europe. The Museum of Modern Art owns books and prints he created. His work has been exhibited in museums in France, Belgium, England and Switzerland. A press release describes his work as large colored acrylics in which the recurring use of geometric figures create abstract compositions that establish a dialogue with one another.

Dan's golf prowess has eroded since he attained a two handicap at the age of 18, but he feels "the rewards of what I'm doing with my career are, of course, an easy tradeoff."

Bill fondly remembers the year he and Dan, then 14 years old, were scheduled to play in the semifinals of the Philadelphia Country Club Better Ball of Partners Championship when Bill had to miss the match to attend a business meeting. According to Bill, "I said to Dan I've never defaulted in a golf tournament yet, and we are not going to do it now. You will have to play them by yourself." Dan had to give his two opponents a stroke on many holes, but he tied them in the 18-hole match and won on the fourth extra hole. Bill and Dan then won the final match the next week.

In 2010, Dan married his longtime girlfriend, Laura Tiozzo, a native of Italy, who has a daughter Cecilia. They live on Long Island.

Laura remembers her first impression of the Walsh family:

"When I was introduced to the family, I was lucky enough to be at a family reunion. As someone outside the family, I was more of an observer. I was really impressed and moved by this family for the incredible values and ethics but also the style. To me as an Italian growing up in Europe, they look like American movie stars. Barbara always looks amazing. She always looks perfect. So there was this beautiful aesthetic aspect that was really something special."

MAURA WALSH BURKE

Her father describes Maura as an outstanding swimmer, and that is an understatement. Of all the talented Walsh swimmers, Maura's accomplishments rank at the highest level.

She won many races at country club and regional meets, then won the Pennsylvania high school championship in the 500-yard freestyle three times while swimming for Harriton High School. "She was deluged with college scholarship offers with calls almost every night at dinner time," Bill remembers. "Finally, she selected the University of Southern California, but there were still frequent calls from colleges trying to get her to change her mind."

Maura certainly justified the USC scholarship, winning the national championship in the 500-yard freestyle and earning All American honors all four years at the university. She twice qualified for the Olympic Trials and felt she had a good chance to make the team in 1980, the year the United States boycotted the Olympics.

While still in college, she became a lifeguard in Huntington Beach, California, and competed successfully in triathlons and half ironman competitions, which combine distance swimming, running and biking. Maura stayed in California for several years, working in sales, before returning to Pennsylvania. She has worked for ECA Recruiters since 1986, explaining, "I strictly place sales and management people in various industries, but mainly I focus on healthcare, academic publishing and medical publishing. I identify clients, I identify candidates, and then I put them together, and I help candidates through the process to get the job." She has consistently ranked among the top producers in her office.

Maura married Kevin Burke, who grew up in the same area as the Walsh children and went to high school with two of the boys. Their son, Brendan is a top all-around athlete at the Haverford School. Their daughter, Ciara, an accomplished Irish step-dancer, attends Country Day School of the Sacred Heart. The Burkes live in Jeffersonville, a Philadelphia suburb.

Kevin, who regularly attends a religious retreat with Bill, said of the hundreds of men at the retreat, "every single one of them" knew Bill's name. "You could tell how respected Bill is," noted Kevin. "He's been a great role model and an inspiration. His spirituality runs deep, and I find that to be compelling."

BRENDAN VINCENT WALSH

From the time he started in the golf business, Brendan set his sights on working at a top-level club. He reached his goal, to say the least, when he became the head golf professional at The Country Club at Brookline, Massachusetts, one of the oldest and most prestigious golf clubs in the United States. The Country Club, one of the five founders of the United States Golf Association, was the setting for Francis Ouimet's historic triumph in the 1913 U.S. Open Championship.

Brendan stood out in sports early, winning three letters in football, basketball and golf at Harriton High School, the most of anyone in his class. He played on the golf team at the College of Wooster in Ohio, graduating with a degree in psychology.

After working as an apprentice golf professional for a summer at the Sankaty Head Golf Club in Nantucket, Brendan turned professional. He worked at clubs in Florida and at the highly rated Ridgewood Country Club in New Jersey, where he helped conduct the U.S. Senior Open Championship before obtaining his first head professional position at The Patterson Club in Fairfield, Connecticut. After spending 1991-97 there, he was hired to take over the helm at The Country Club.

When The Country Club served as the venue for the 1999 Ryder Cup Matches between the United States and Europe, Brendan was able to secure tickets for Bill and Barbara, and some of his siblings were on hand as volunteers as the United States emerged victorious with a thrilling rally. "Dad was so excited about his experience," Brendan recalls, "that he started to share his story with his various organizations. He kept calling me for programs so he could give them out. He must have purchased five hundred before it was all said and done."

Brendan's schedule allows him to take his wife, Desiree, daughter Audrey Rose and twin daughters Caroline Grace and Gabrielle Christina to visit Bill and Barbara in Florida during the winter. "Because of my time in Florida," Brendan said, "I have had the chance to meet a lot of people through my dad, which has opened up a lot of doors along the way in my career. To be able to spend this time with him and see how he carries himself as a person has helped me both personally and professionally."

His daughters are following his childhood interest in sports. "I'm back and forth to the club three or four times a day," he noted, "because I'm going to their soccer, basketball or lacrosse games. I've even coached their teams, and I love it."

PAUL ANTHONY WALSH ("CHET")

The Hardy Boys books were popular when the Walsh boys were growing up. The older boys, Michael and Matt, gave out nicknames based on the characters. Paul was called "Chet," and that moniker is still with him.

Chet became the best golfer in a family of fine golfers, carrying a plus-four handicap at one time. He was the golf and basketball captain his junior and senior years at Harriton High School. Later he coached the freshman basketball team at Harriton and the junior varsity and varsity teams at Archbishop Carroll High School. Chet received the first golf scholarship awarded by Villanova and went on to serve as assistant coach and head coach of the golf team there. He won the Big East championship as a team member in 1985 and as the coach in 1990. He is believed to be the only individual with that distinction. He was the first golfer to be inducted into the Villanova Varsity Club Hall of Fame in February 2011.

While succeeding at the highest levels of amateur golf, Chet has worked in the golf car industry, currently as a regional manager for Golf Car Specialties, based in Pottstown, Pennsylvania.

He remembers playing golf at the age of six at Philadelphia Country Club. He honed his skills on the "Walsh Valley" course created by brothers Tim and Dan in their backyard. Chet is a remarkably good partner, having paired with numerous players to win more than 15 different team events in the Philadelphia area. He recalls teaming with brother Tim to win an invitational tournament at Philadelphia Cricket Club, while he and his father won several Golf Association of Philadelphia Father and Son Championships. He and Tom Shallow Jr., a lifelong friend and fellow Philadelphia Country Club member, won the prestigious Baltusrol Invitational at the renowned Baltusrol Golf Club in New Jersey. Individually, Chet has qualified to play in eight United States Golf Association championships, and he has been low amateur three times in the Philadelphia Open Championship. He has won the Horace Rawlins Invitational at The Springhaven Club nine times.

Chet also has won 10 Philadelphia Country Club championships, although he intended to stop at seven, the total his father won. When Bill heard about the plan, he insisted that Chet keep competing.

Chet and his wife Cindy have two daughters, Delaney and Bridget (named for Chet's sister), and a son, William Thomas Walsh II. They live in Wayne, a Philadelphia suburb.

Chet Walsh considers the 1995 George Arthur Crump Cup at Pine Valley Golf Club his most significant victory in golf. Leading amateurs from around the United States competed at this golf course, generally ranked as the best in the world.

He and Bill McGuinness were tied after 11 holes in the final 18-hole match when Chet hit his drive on the 12th hole wildly into the woods. "Blocked by a tree, he had no play," reported a history of Philadelphia golf, "unless he could carve a low and viciously slicing shot that would somehow manage to skip and skim its way onto the narrow green." Chet could not pull off that miraculous shot and sent the ball instead into a sand hazard 75 feet from the hole. Chet's recollection of his next shot: "I said to myself, 'Just get it on the green and keep Billy honest here. Don't let him have an easy two-putt win.' The next thing you know, the ball goes in the hole."

Chet won the hole and the match.

ANDREW THOMAS WALSH ("BUCK")

Buck is generally considered the joker of the Walsh family. It was he who first called his father "Sarge" and his mother "Bubs." Explains Buck: "I was the one who started teasing my father and making fun of his regimental ways. It was probably a combination of me being a bit of a goofball and him becoming a bit softer in his old age."

Like his brothers, Buck was a good athlete, but his father said he did not have their intensity to win: "He was more interested in making his teammates laugh." Buck played football and basketball at Harriton High School.

As a sophomore at Hobart College in upstate New York, Buck was selected as an exchange student to the University of Bath, south of London. "He liked it so much," his father recalls, "that he never went back to Hobart. Instead he talked the University of Bath officials into accepting him as a permanent student." Following graduation, he served for a year as the graduate representative supervising faculty-student relations. Buck liked England so much that after two years back in the United States, he was able to arrange employment in London. He has since added a British citizenship to his United States citizenship.

"I love it over here," Buck said of his decision to remain abroad. "I think even my parents were scratching their heads at first when I told them I wanted to stay here permanently, but now to them it's just another far-off place where one of their children lives. We're all over the place, aren't we? There's bound to be one of us living abroad."

Buck worked 10 years for HSBC, one of the world's largest banking and financial services companies, and is now an institutional stock broker with Societe Generale, a major global financial services company based in France.

Bill and Barbara and several of Buck's siblings were in Oslo, Norway, for his wedding to Thea, a Norwegian woman. They live in the Kensington section of London with their daughter Nora and their son Lars.

ALEXANDRA FRENCH WALSH ("LEXA")

Lexa may be the youngest of the Walsh children, but she has compiled a remarkable list of occupations and activities in a relatively short time. She graduated from Harriton High School and from the California College of Arts and Crafts and 20 years later resumed her studies as a graduate student at Portland State University in Oregon.

"In the interim," Lexa noted, "I have been a practicing artist, musician, world traveler, volunteer arts administrator-curator and English teacher in the Czech Republic, interior designer and organizer (definitely a trait developed from Sarge at an early age). And I fancy myself a darn good cook, even though it drives me crazy that Sarge won't eat garlic."

In the Czech Republic, she volunteered at an art center for eight summers, returning to California in the winters. She relates the experience to "our upbringing of community service."

At Portland State, she studied Art and Social Practice, which is art using social interaction as the medium. She put this degree to work as the Portland Art Museum's first Artist-in-Residence.

"I would like to be a professor in a program like the one at PSU," Lexa said. "But I also just want to make more compelling art projects.

My artwork has transformed from sculpture to being more social, public and participatory. When I discovered this program, it seemed like it was meant for me. Now I can place myself in art history and see where I stand. Nowadays an artist has a lot of roles, not just to sit in her studio and paint."

Growing up, Lexa made two firm pronouncements. First she did not want to be an athlete like so many of her siblings, so she stopped golfing at the age of 12.

Second, she promised her father she would never get married. That commitment lasted until 2009 when she married Dan Nelson in California with most of her family present. Her father was disappointed the wedding did not take place in a Catholic church but commented that "the quiet little outdoor setting among the redwood trees was beautiful and the judge who performed the ceremony did a wonderful job."

"Gash sakes," Bill told the judge, "you're not a priest, but I like you."

CHAPTER 16

Everyone Is Different

The 15 Walsh children are definitely not of one mind, but they agree unanimously that as Brendan puts it: "Our family is very open to one another. We do have our differences, but everybody cares, and everybody loves one another, and we will always be there to try to help."

Adds Buck: "Despite how different we all are, we still have a great mutual appreciation of each other."

Here are comments on the siblings' relationship from other members of the family:

Lexa: The most beautiful thing about our family is our love and tolerance for our diversity of lifestyles, politics, spirituality, etc. I'm probably one of the most left-leaning people in the family, and I think it's wonderful that I can have a discussion with, say, Maura's husband, Kevin, who is very, very, very, very "right," but he's willing to go into it, and we can pat each other on the back at the end. So instead of it being like a fighting match about trying to convince each other that the other is right, we are just willing to have an intellectual discussion. I think we all say, "You're my family, and we're part of this unique, wonderful family." We love each other, and that's the most important thing. If only the world could be that way.

Bridget: I know so many people who can't stand to be in the same room with their siblings. They talk about the awful experience they're about to have at Christmas if they have to sit across the dinner table from their sister or brother or whomever. One thing that can be said about this family—you can't really describe how we all get together so well and how we jump in and out of each other's conversations. It's just a real sight to behold.

Chet: What makes the Walsh family so unique? The biggest thing is we all get along, yet we're not a family that has to talk to everybody every day, every week. I could go months at a time without talking to my brothers and sisters, but it's no big deal. When you see them the next time, it's like you never missed a beat.

Matt: To go to these family reunions, it's a wonderful thing. It's heart-warming, the fact that there's so much togetherness. There's no kid in our family that's really revolted against the system or that can say they don't like other people in the family. I can't say there's any instance where there's one kid that doesn't like another person.

Stephanie: There's nobody who doesn't like to be in the family or with the family. No black sheep, nobody who's sort of remote or anything. Everybody wants to be with everybody. You don't find that very often. We know a lot of families with a lot of kids who grew up with us, and either they're the black sheep, or they have sisters who are just off somewhere and don't come home for holidays or weddings or anything like that, and that's kind of sad.

Maura: We all get along, and most importantly, we respect each other for who we are. For the most part, we love being together. I enjoy being with my family. Even when we don't agree, I still love being with them, I really do.

Monica: The amazing thing about our family is that I think that we've all turned out well, we're all healthy, we're all doing well, and none of us has had any serious problems anywhere. That's not to say there haven't been challenges here and there, but we're all functioning, healthy people who are out there in the world, doing what means a lot to us. I think the most important thing is that we're very personable as a family. If anyone meets us as a family or separately, they're moved by our genuineness, our willingness to be helpful and to engage and to just be conscious, loving people. And I think to have that in a family of 15 kids is a pretty amazing thing.

Michael: The uniqueness of our family is that we are all really different. Each person has his or her own personality. As we're getting older, I think we're really appreciating our time together. When we have our Thanksgivings and our Christmases and when we're with our parents, they remind us that it is really important that we have this time together. Bottom line, we really love and respect each other very much.

Bill and Barbara with all 15 of their children during
their 25th wedding anniversary celebration at the
house on Booth Lane in Haverford in 1973.

The Walsh family celebrates Christmas on Booth Lane in 1980.

The Swimmin' Walsh Women, from left: Stephanie, Minna, Bridget, Monica, Tez, Huddie, Maura and Lexa.

Bill and Barbara enjoyed dancing on Thursday nights at Philadelphia Country Club.

The Walsh home on Booth Lane contained countless
memories of a lively family growing up.

Skytop Lodge was the setting for the family to celebrate
Bill's and Barbara's 60th wedding anniversary in 2008.
(Photo by V.I.P. Studios, Inc., Ken Schurman.)

CHAPTER 17

Retreating to Malvern

Bill Walsh is the author of this chapter.

When I was at Villanova, I attended a few religious retreats held on the campus but given by an Augustinian who did not reside at Villanova. (They wanted it to be someone we didn't know.) Later on I was talked into going to a few others in Morristown, New Jersey when we resided in Plainfield.

After living in the Philadelphia area for less than a year, I was approached by a man I had met at church to attend a weekend retreat at Malvern Retreat House, a beautiful 125-acre countryside estate purchased in the early 1920s by a group of Catholic men in the Philadelphia Archdiocese. They wanted to have a private place where religious retreats could be held free of all the noise of a regular parish church.

I attended and was extremely impressed, and I have been very active ever since, receiving my 50-year pin in 2007. I have never come home from our annual retreat, held either on the first or the second weekend in March, without feeling that I was a better husband, a better father and a better all-around Catholic as a result of the weekend.

Having been the captain of our Holy Family Group and serving two different terms totaling 15 years on the Retreat's Board of Directors, I feel

I can genuinely attest to the benefits these weekend retreats mean to so many families.

The startling thing is that Malvern Retreat, which is celebrating its 100th year in 2012, receives no financial support from the Philadelphia Archdiocese. All expenses are covered by the generosity of those people who attend. (They have married-couple and single-woman retreats now, a recent change and a popular one.) Certain business and religious organizations are also hosted for one-week retreats.

The added benefit for our children back when they were young was that each year I'd come home with some sort of gift for each of them (rosary, holy cards, medals, books, etc.) with the next oldest (who had not yet received a nice, thick prayer book) receiving one—something they "worshipped"—and the younger ones waited their turn to receive one.

Malvern Retreat House has an Archdiocesan priest in residence with occasional changes being made by the reigning cardinal. In the early 1990s, the appointee to the Retreat position was Father Dennis O'Donnell. Besides becoming a very close friend of Barbara's and mine and our family members, he did an excellent job at the Retreat House, and many other retreatants feel about him as our family does. I made five retreats given by him of my 55 total at Malvern, and those five are the best I have ever made. And each year of the five has been even better than the previous one.

Our family thinks so highly of him that we have invited him to our 50th and 60th wedding anniversary celebrations held at different locations about two hours from Philadelphia in the Poconos.

While there, he says Mass, participates in the golf tournament and the other events and spends a lot of time talking with our children and grandchildren.

After spending 12 years at Malvern Retreat House, Father Denny, as we call him, received permission to start an orphanage in Honduras in his "spare time," something he really wanted to do. With a lot of help from his friends and retreatants, he was extremely successful. The name of the orphanage is Amigos de Jesus, and it has been a great source of satisfaction to him.

As it grew, however, the orphanage took more and more of his time, and he and the Retreat House Board agreed that he would be released from his duties in Malvern so he could spend an unlimited amount of time in Honduras. While we hated to have him leave the Retreat House, he still gives five or six retreats a year there, and in fact he gave the one a few days before my 85th birthday (March 23, 2007) with all our sons and many of our grandsons and sons-in-law present. It was a wonderful, religious weekend, and his giving the retreat with so many of our family and acquaintances there was a complete surprise to me, as was the party on that Sunday evening with all the females in the family included.

Along with his orphanage responsibilities and half-dozen other retreats at Malvern, Father Denny gives retreats at parishes in the area and in Florida. While in the Philadelphia area, he lives at Holy Redeemer Hospital in Huntingdon Valley and serves in a religious capacity there.

After Father Denny's departure as rector, the Retreat House hired a salaried president. It is being run very well and in a much more business-like fashion. Jim Fitzsimmons, formerly a vice president at Temple, is the president. Jim has had much success in bringing new groups to Malvern Retreat during the week when space is readily available.

Malvern Retreat has a quarterly publication that is sent out to all retreatants. It includes photos and articles about groups that had been on retreat during the previous quarter. It published the following commentary by Father Denny after our 50th wedding anniversary in September of 1998, which we celebrated with him in the eastern Poconos at Woodloch Springs.

Taking The Time To Say Thank You

A few months ago I was asked by a married couple to celebrate Mass for them on the occasion of their 50th wedding anniversary. Besides the wonderful friendship I share with them, I was looking forward to meeting their entire family for the first time — all 15 of their sons and daughters along with in-laws and grandchildren.

While I looked forward to the Mass, I was a little anxious because no thoughts were coming to me for a homily, and I wanted to be able to offer a decent homily. In fact, as we sat down to begin Mass, my mind was still blank. Now for many priests this can be a very dangerous thing because somewhere in priests' school a dangerous imp has whispered in all priests' minds that if you just talk long enough, something good would come out. Fortunately, at this Eucharistic celebration I did not give in to the temptation.

And so at the time for the homily, I mentioned the simple truth that we were gathered at the "Eucharistic" Table of the Lord—a Greek word that means Thanksgiving. I asked the 15 children if there was anything for which they wanted to thank God and their parents. In two seconds I realized why the Lord did not give me any thoughts for a homily, for it only took two seconds for the first daughter to say for what she thanked God and her parents.

"I want to thank God and my parents for showing us the love they had for each other was first. We knew they loved us, but we knew it was because they first loved each other." She then talked about her parents' "date night" every week—not a small task with 15 children. The second speaker was a son who thanked them for setting clear moral guidelines and clear sanctions when the goals were crossed. There was a little laughter over the "sanctions" part (I guess you had to be one of the family to appreciate that, especially when many of the children call the father "Sarge") until the third sibling said, "But we always knew we were loved and our family was there for us no matter how badly we crossed the line."

The "homily" went on with similar sentiments, and as I sat there with this large, wonderful family, I thought of what was not being said. No one thanked these parents for cars, clothes, golf clubs, education or bank accounts—the "things" many of us worry about for our children—the "things" we want to give them that "we never had." And in focusing on those "things," we miss the really important matters of life—the things we did have growing up—integrity, love, humor, trust, faith—the things for which these 15 children were thanking their parents.

About a month after the Mass, one of the daughters wrote me to thank me for giving them the opportunity to express their gratitude to their parents and tell them how much they love them. She then said, "They already know that but it was good to say it." In each of our lives there are many people we want to thank and tell them how much we love them—we are "sure they know it," but why wait for a 50th anniversary Mass to say it? Today there is a phone that can be picked up, a letter that can be written or a quiet moment we could spend with someone we love and for whom we are eternally grateful—to simply say that which we hope they know—thank you.

Father Denny talked about the Walsh family and his work in Honduras during an interview early in 2011:

The one thing that strikes me with the family is that all 15 children are completely unique, that Bill and Barbara have given them wonderful roots and structures, but they've also given them wonderful wings to fly. They're just a very healthy, balanced family and also very creative.

Everyone knows that Barbara is the quiet person in the background who makes things happen, who puts everything together. Bill obviously has provided the healthy structure and everything for the family.

Bill and Barbara have been very generous [to the orphanage in Honduras]. You know every month on this day you'll be getting a check from Bill and Barbara Walsh. And they've been a huge help to the children.

The orphanage is doing great. It's 12 years old, and we just keep building. We just finished building the school, and we're about to build the girls' residence. Right now we have about 60 boys. I would expect in two years to have 180. Other people have come to us, so we're helping other orphanages in South America and in Africa. We're also helping some girls' orphanages in Honduras, so all together we're taking care of about 500 kids right now. It's a great thing. It's fantastic.

Father Denny was playing with Bill, Barbara and Chet in the family golf tournament held as part of the couple's 50th wedding anniversary celebration. "This one hole had a really steep hill off the fairway," Father Denny recalls, "and Barbara sliced it down the hill. She had just had a hip operation, so Chet said, 'don't go down there. I'll get the ball for you,' which was nice. You kind of expect that from your kid. And he put the ball down and said, 'Now you're lying four.' He penalized her two strokes. He said, 'If you had gone down there, Mom, I wouldn't have penalized you.' So they're really sticklers for honesty, I guess you would say."

CHAPTER 18

Bill and the Knights

Along with his faithful participation in the retreats and his local Catholic church, Bill Walsh became a member and supporter of two other charitable Catholic organizations, the Knights of Columbus and the Knights of the Holy Sepulchre.

Bill was invited to join the Knights of Columbus while living in Plainfield, New Jersey. He pointed out, "The Knights of Columbus Council not only gives a good amount of money to charity, but the members also take the time to do many helpful things for people who are handicapped, underprivileged or in need of the help of others. One of the activities that impressed me immensely was the taking of disabled war veterans to Mass on Sundays. Our council did this weekly with the responsibility being shifted among 24 different members. We also attended a weekend religious retreat in the spring of each year at a Jesuit retreat house in Morristown, New Jersey. Our council was also deeply involved in Plainfield and North Plainfield civic activities."

Bill was elected Grand Knight of the council and in 1954 received the Fourth Degree, the highest degree of the organization. The purpose of the Fourth Degree is to foster the spirit of patriotism and encourage active Catholic citizenship.

When the Walsh family moved to the Philadelphia area, Bill was accepted into a new Knights of Columbus council in suburban Narberth, but his busy work schedule limited his participation. The Supreme Council in New Haven, Connecticut, made him a Life Member at age 65. "I have always regretted that I couldn't be more active in the organization because of all the good it does and the effectiveness of its many meaningful endeavors all over the world."

Bill was invited to join the The Equestrian Order of the Holy Sepulchre of Jerusalem (Knights of the Holy Sepulchre) by a friend, John Rouse. The Order is charged with providing for the needs of the Latin Patriarchate of Jerusalem and for all the activities and initiatives necessary to support the Christian presence in the Holy Land. The contributions made by its members throughout the world are the main source of funding.

With the endorsement of his local pastor, Father Jim Martinez, Bill was accepted and scheduled for induction at St. Patrick's Cathedral in New York City on September 26, 1992, with a dinner scheduled the night before the induction and a luncheon following it, both at the Waldorf-Astoria. "I realized that this new organization, as prestigious as it appeared to be, was also going to be fairly expensive."

Another issue: the induction was planned for 11 a.m., and Bill was scheduled to play in the Philadelphia Country Club Super Senior (age 65 and over) Championship final round at 2 p.m. that day. Bill skipped the dinner and luncheon, attended the Mass at St. Patrick's and the induction, then dashed for his car. "It was going to be close," he recalls.

Bill drove to the club in a heavy rainstorm, arriving at 1:45 and was beginning to change into golf clothes only to learn it had been raining since dawn. The club decided the course was too wet to complete the championship and declared Bill the winner. (He had been leading by five strokes.)

"What a strange ending to a busy, fast-driving day. I had left home for New York City at seven o'clock that morning. Though I felt a little guilty about putting the induction behind a golf tournament in importance, I did appreciate what John Rouse had done for me. Because all the functions were held in New York City or Jerusalem, I have never been very active in the Order."

CHAPTER 19

Bill's View on Religion

Bill Walsh is the author of this chapter.

There is no doubt in my mind that when I was a young boy, there seemed to be a lot more emphasis placed on religious education than there is today.

Of course, I was in Catholic schools up through college, so in those days, we were taught largely by nuns and priests. Many of them were very strict, and they generally conveyed the message that if we died with a mortal sin on our soul without getting to a priest for confession, we would go straight to hell. This put a lot of fear into our hearts and probably made us better kids than we would otherwise have been.

Nowadays, a lot of young people don't even believe there is a God, let alone hell. While this can be debated ad infinitum, and I am a strong believer in a person's right to believe as he or she wishes, I am thankful that I believe as I do and that I married someone who believed the same way.

In our own family, despite what Barbara and I believe and have tried to have them, by our example, follow suit, only about half of our children and grandchildren regularly attend Mass on Sundays and Holy Days. It is my principal daily prayer to get the rest of them back going to Mass and Communion on at least a weekly basis.

Not to brag about my religious habits, but to make the point that they are important to me, I have been going to daily Mass and Communion since the summer of 1946, when I returned home from the South Pacific. If you allow for a few days a year (no Mass on Good Friday, occasional travel to places that don't have Mass during the week), I'll assume that I have attended Mass more than 23,500 times (1946 to 2011, 360 times a year, including Holy Days).

That's a lot of Masses. In addition, I have attended 55 annual retreats at Malvern Retreat House, and I say the Rosary every day.

I mention this not only for the repeated attention of our children and grandchildren but also to show that I have no doubt that what I have been doing is the right thing to do because it brings me closer to God.

Does He always give me what I am praying for? Certainly not. A priest told me a long time ago that we should pray not for what we want, but for what God wants us to have—in other words, put our wishes in harmony with God's. Once we really believe in this concept, we are never really disappointed over not getting something we really thought we wanted.

Think of all the depression and disappointment that we would avoid if we could just accept this principle. It applies to all phases of life, in getting a job, finding a wife or husband, receiving a promotion, or even wanting to win a golf tournament, a basketball, football or baseball game or any athletic contest. The principle remains the same—do everything that is fair and honest that we can do, and I mean going all out for what we want and not being half-hearted about it. But if we don't receive it, despite our effort and prayer, accept the fact that God didn't think it was best for us, at least at that time, and move on with our lives. We will be much happier, and God will see that we are taken care of in another manner.

Admittedly, this may seem too simple, but believe me, it does work, and we are always happy because we are putting our lives in God's hands—a foolproof way to live.

If a determined effort to get what we want is combined with a lot of confident prayer, life will always be bearable, even if our desired objective is not immediately realized.

CHAPTER 20

Loyalty to Villanova

While Villanova University has been significant through the years to Bill Walsh, it is also fair to say that Bill has been very important to Villanova.

From the time of his graduation in the class of 1943 until the family moved to the Philadelphia area in 1955, Bill says he was "a mostly disinterested alumnus." Following the move, his interest intensified as did his support and alumni leadership. He and family members became regulars at Villanova football and basketball games, Bill increased his financial contributions, he became active in the Villanova Club of Philadelphia and in alumni activities.

He served as club president in 1960-62, president of the nationwide General Alumni Association in 1971-72 and as a member of the University Development Council from 1968 to 1990. All this service led to high honors from the university. The College of Commerce and Finance, from which Bill graduated, appointed him a member of the school's Board of Visitors for an indefinite term. He received the Villanova Alumni Award in 1969. And he received the Villanova Loyalty Award, given for unending loyalty throughout the years to Villanova. It is the university's oldest award, dating to 1932, and is considered the most exclusive recognition. *(Winners of the Loyalty Award appear as an appendix.)*

As the 1968 winner of the Loyalty Award, Bill had the responsibility of arranging the 1969 dinner for the past honorees and to select the current winner. The dinner took place at the Picket Post near Villanova. "A few months after the dinner," Bill recalls, "I received a call from Bill Schubert, Class of 1942, a very prominent alumnus and a close friend from our time together at Penn Law School, saying that the group was so impressed with the way the dinner had been handled that they wanted me to take the job permanently. What could I say? So here it is, more than 40 years later, and I'm still doing the job."

Bill credits Ruth Bugglin, his longtime secretary in the insurance office, "a loyal, hardworking lady," for taking over most of the details involved in planning the dinners. "She once said to me, 'How come you accept all these jobs, and I end up doing all the work, and you get all the credit?' I think she was joking." Miss Bugglin, as she was known, retired to Arizona in 1965 but returned for part-time work a few years later.

Villanova capped its recognition of Bill Walsh with a Doctor of Humane Letters degree. Bill will always remember that he received his doctorate in 1985—that's the year Villanova pulled off its stunning upset of Georgetown to win the NCAA basketball championship.

"I still do a few things for Villanova other than take care of the Loyalty Award," Bill notes, "and the progress of the university in so many different ways has been wonderful to see."

Villanova is the owner and beneficiary of a permanent life insurance policy Bill purchased in 1971 that has a death benefit of more than $200,000. Three of the Walsh sons, Michael, Matthew and Chet, and Matt's sons, Matt Jr. and Greg, also have graduated from Villanova.

CHAPTER 21

"Service Above Self"

An invitation in 1970 to join the Rotary Club of Ardmore, Pennsylvania started another significant chapter in Bill Walsh's career that continues to this day. As a Rotarian holding leadership positions, he followed the career of his father, who served as president of Rotary clubs in Metuchen, New Jersey and New York City and as district governor of Manhattan County. Bill also followed the path of his sponsor in the Ardmore club, George Uhlig. Both were presidents of the club and district governors for Southeastern Pennsylvania. Uhlig also was a director and vice president of Rotary International.

Rotary clubs meet once a week. The Ardmore club's day is Thursday. Rotarians are expected to attend at least 60 percent of the meetings, and quite a few strive for 100 percent. If they cannot make a meeting of their home club, they may attend a Rotary meeting anywhere in the world within two weeks of the club date they missed and receive attendance credit.

"While this attendance requirement is a deterrent with some prospective members," Bill explained, "in the long run, it is what keeps Rotary such a strong, vibrant organization. The requirement means that attending meetings is very important in getting members much more involved and in realizing the pleasure and satisfaction one gets from being an active part of a project that means so much to a town, a region, a small group or even a family that is being helped by the Rotarians' effort."

Bill has more than 40 years of perfect attendance. "If God lets me live long enough, I hope to reach 50 years."

Rotary took on the challenge of wiping out polio by the year 2005, 100 years after the founding of Rotary International. The Ardmore club contributed $200,000 to the program, second in the district only to the larger Philadelphia club.

While the campaign was remarkably successful, there are still some polio cases where vaccines were not permitted, so Rotary is still pushing eradication and trying to overcome the politics in the objecting countries.

"Rotary is a wonderful organization," according to Bill. "It not only does wonderful things for humanity, it makes those who take an active part in campaigns like polio eradication feel wonderful, too. I highly recommend membership in Rotary.

"I can't say enough about most of the Rotarians I have met in my life. They are sincerely interested in helping those less fortunate than themselves, both with time spent on Rotary's many projects throughout the world and financially. While we do a lot of charitable work in Rotary, we also have a lot of fun, develop many good friendships and have many good times socially."

The motto of Rotary International is "Service Above Self."

The Object of Rotary

The Object of Rotary is to encourage and foster the ideal of service as a basis of worthy enterprise and, in particular, to encourage and foster:

FIRST, The development of acquaintance as an opportunity for service;

SECOND, High ethical standards in business and professions, the recognition of the worthiness of all useful occupations, and the dignifying of each Rotarian's occupation as an opportunity to serve society;

THIRD, The application of the ideal of service in each Rotarian's personal, business, and community life;

FOURTH, The advancement of international understanding, goodwill, and peace through a world fellowship of business and professional persons united in the ideal of service.

The Rotary Four-Way Test

Of the things we think, say or do:

1. Is it the TRUTH?
2. Is it FAIR to all concerned?
3. Will it build GOODWILL and BETTER FRIENDSHIPS?
4. Will it be BENEFICIAL to all concerned?

Bill Walsh recounts a trip he enjoyed with three Ardmore Rotarians:

In May, 1980, 10 years after I joined Ardmore Rotary, a fellow Rotarian, Norm Rothenhaber, who was a member of the same church I was, Our Mother of Good Counsel, asked me if I would join him, Bob Wood and Ralph Warren on a golfing trip to Scotland in early July.

I told Norm that I'd love to go, but that I'd have to clear it with Barbara. I think Barbara, bless her heart, was more excited than even I was about playing those famous Scottish golf courses, and she said I should go.

Norm was pleased that the foursome was now complete. He asked me if I would room with him in Scotland. He was a very nice older man, 77 at the time. Norm noticed a somewhat perplexed look on my face, I guess, and said 'You're the only other Catholic in the group, and I want to make sure I'm with someone who will make sure that a priest will be called in case I have a heart attack.' I told him that I would room with him on one condition, that he would not smoke a cigar in the room. He agreed that he would not.

The trip was a magnificent experience. Our wives waved goodbye to us as we boarded the plane, and after a short stop in Boston, we arrived in Glasgow the next morning at 6:30 a.m. and went directly to the famous Turnberry Hotel, which sits beautifully at the top of a lofty hill overlooking the highly regarded Turnberry Ailsa golf course.

We found out there was an early evening Mass close by so we decided to play golf early, completely going back on our original resolve to get some sleep before we played golf. By the time we got to the second green, we weren't even tired any more. As I recall, I shot 81 that first day. Norm and I made Mass on time and then joined Bob and Ralph at the hotel for dinner. The meals there were excellent and the desserts unforgettable.

The next morning our starting time was 10:40 a.m. so we were able to catch up a bit on lost sleep. I was quite happy with my 77.

After another delicious dinner and a good night's sleep, we played Prestwick, the site of the first 24 British Opens. It was not, to me at least, as good a golf course as Turnberry but still very enjoyable to play. I shot an even 80.

That afternoon we played another fine course, Royal Troon, a famous layout not far away from the Turnberry Hotel. It was a good test of golf. I would rank it slightly behind Turnberry and ahead of Prestwick.

On each of the first two evenings Norm had refrained from eating any sweets, having fruit instead. We kidded him so much about it that he finally agreed to have chocolate cake and ice cream that night. The only problem was, respecting his age, we passed him the cake and told him he could take as big a piece as he wanted because he hadn't had any the first two nights. He shocked us—he ate the entire cake himself plus a fair amount of ice cream. We had to order another cake. Our waiter was as surprised as we were.

Our Wednesday schedule called for no golf, only bus travel to a hotel near St. Andrews and stops at a clothing shop and one dealing in Scottish souvenirs on the way. Though all of us would have preferred to be playing golf, we were stuck with the planned itinerary, so we bought a few souvenirs and suffered through the trip. We arrived at the hotel at about 3 p.m. and were able to watch the Olympics on television. They were being held in Russia, but because the U.S. had refused to participate, we couldn't really cheer for anyone.

That night's dinner at the new hotel wasn't as good as those of our first three evenings, but it wasn't bad. The thing we didn't do, however, was pass the cake to Norm. Whether it was all the cake he ate the night before or the bus ride, he wasn't too chipper that night at dinner.

On Thursday morning we played the Old Course at St. Andrews and that afternoon tackled the New Course.

The Old Course was much different from any course I had ever played. It was certainly memorable. I actually scored better at the more difficult course with a 75 and shot 77 in the afternoon on the New Course.

Our Friday itinerary found us at Carnoustie, another frequent site for the British Open. I actually felt that it was the most difficult of the courses we had played, and though I shot an 80, felt very good about it.

Our last course was at Gleneagles, another fine hotel and home of the King's Course, which we played, and the Queen's Course, which we were told was somewhat easier. We were all a little tired by this time, I guess—our final round in Scotland—as I had an 83 on a course quite a bit easier than Carnoustie.

That evening the travel company that arranged the trip had a closing dinner featuring haggis, reportedly the best meat dish in Scotland. With all due respect to the Scots' taste, I feel that haggis was the worst meal I ever had in my life.

We boarded our plane the next morning in Glasgow and arrived safely back in Philadelphia that afternoon, relishing the good time we had but happy to be home with our families.

Though I went on other Rotary trips when I was president of the Ardmore Club (New Orleans) and district governor (London and Kansas City), none had the enjoyable memories of that trip to Scotland.

Unfortunately, Norm Rothenhaber died the day after he celebrated his 99th birthday. Bob Wood had died 10 years earlier, and Ralph Warren died shortly after Norm, at age 78. We became very close friends on that trip, and I miss them all.

CHAPTER 22

Thoughts from Friends

Friends of Bill Walsh interviewed for this book spoke in glowing terms about his character, integrity, ethics, faith, thoughtfulness and generosity. They noted his competitiveness and willingness to exchange barbs. In a word, they found him remarkable.

Here are some excerpts from the interviews:

Mike Greenberg, golfing friend, companion at Malvern Retreats: Bill is a gentleman who would do anything for anybody. He's really motivated me to do things he's seen in me beyond what I would have thought I would do in my lifetime. I think of him like I do my dad. I have a lot of respect and love for Bill. In regard to his family, I think they're probably my pick for the All-American family.

Craig Lundberg, past president of the Golf Association of Philadelphia: Bill's a very predictable person. You know where Bill is all the time. He is himself. He never puts on airs. He never pretends to be more than he is, just a straightforward, honest, consistent friend. He's such a wonderful guy. He's widely admired.

Ken Warren, longtime friend and partner in member-guest tournaments at Philadelphia Country Club, Merion, Pine Valley and St.

Davids golf clubs: Bill is very kind to everybody that he meets. He would come up to you and introduce himself, not in a trying-to-sell-insurance way or anything of that sort. He's easy to talk to, and he would always have something good to say. If he didn't have anything good to say about you, he wouldn't say it.

Arch Waldman, past secretary-treasurer of the Golf Association of Philadelphia who was interviewed before his death in 2011: Because of my involvement with GAP, I met Bill and Craig Lundberg, and we have kept in touch with one another for 30 years. Bill is a very, very hardened Catholic, Craig is a Protestant who was born in North Dakota, and I was a poor Jewish boy from West Philadelphia. I always found it interesting that three people from such different backgrounds would find a friendship that has lasted many, many years. Bill is very dogged. He sets goals that may seem preposterous—and he always meets them. You can go a long, long time before you meet somebody like Bill.

Stan Friedman, co-winner with Bill of the Golf Association of Philadelphia Distinguished Service Award and a longtime friend who was interviewed before his death in 2011: Bill's a man of tremendously strong character. He has the courage of his convictions, and he absolutely stands for courage and truth. He has qualities that make him beloved. He's truly one of my best and dearest friends. He's a man of tremendous faith. I'm totally at peace with the world when I'm with him.

Stan Engle, past president of Philadelphia Country Club and Jupiter Hills Golf Club, longtime friend: In the more than 30 years that I've known Bill, I've never heard one negative word about the guy. He's the kind of guy who, from a golf perspective, I would never think about whether or not he would call an infraction upon himself or cause an infraction. He's just the type of person that you know he'll do the right thing at all times.

He and I trade barbs all the time like he does with everybody, and he's pretty good at it. I think he takes exception if you don't give it back to him. We're playing at Philly Country one day, and he and I had been going at each other pretty good. This mutual friend of ours who had never played with the two of us together says, 'If I didn't know you guys were good friends, I'd feel that I'd have to step between the two of you.' I remember

I once said to Barbara, 'Sometimes I think I do this too much.' She said, 'Don't ever stop. He'll think there's something wrong.' That's just part of his nature.

Stafford Gellatly, longtime golfing companion of Bill's at Jupiter Hills: Bill is a first-class gentleman, but he's a pain in the neck as a golfer because he always takes money from you. He bets everybody the same amount, a $2 Nassau. His concentration on the golf course when everybody's fooling around is fundamental. It's one of the main reasons he plays such a good game.

Stan Friedman said of Bill "He's the toughest competitor I've ever played golf with or against. He has the sharpest needle in the world." Friedman recalled playing a match at Philadelphia Country Club with Tim DeBaufre, the club professional, as his partner against Bill and his son Matt:

"On either the 14th or 15th hole, my tee ball goes in a bunker 198 yards from the green. I hit a 4-iron, the sweetest shot I ever hit in my life, and it's almost a leaner. DeBaufre jumps out of his shoes. 'What a great golf shot!' Everybody's patting me on the back, but do you know what Bill said to me—'I can't believe a man with your limited ability could hit a shot that well.' "

The Walsh family was synonymous with golf at Philadelphia Country Club. With Bill is Chet, who became the best golfer in the family.

Bill ranks the Philadelphia Senior Amateur Championship in 1991 as his top golfing achievement. (photo by Carol Kodsi.)

Taking part in an exhibition at Philadelphia Country Club for its 75th anniversary, from left: club professional Loma Frakes, Bill Walsh, Hall of Fame golfer Byron Nelson, who won the U.S. Open at the club in 1939, and Helen Sigel Wilson, a club member and one of the greatest women golfers in Philadelphia history.

Bill and his seven sons toured the great golf courses of Ireland in honor of his 75th birthday in 1997. From left are Tim, Matt, Chet, Bill, Dan, Mike, Brendan and Buck.

CHAPTER 23

The Walsh Open

For more than half a century, Bill Walsh's golf experiences have been intertwined with the club generally considered the best golf course in the world—Pine Valley Golf Club.

George Arthur Crump, a Philadelphia hotelier, discovered the Pine Valley land near Clementon, New Jersey and not far from Philadelphia. It took vast imagination to envision a golf course on the thickly wooded, forbidding 183 acres (since expanded to more than 600 acres) that Crump purchased in 1913. Yet consulting with some of the leading golf architects of the day, Crump produced a memorable, challenging course that publications have consistently ranked number one in the world.

Soon after Bill arrived in Philadelphia, a business associate, Mel Dickenson Jr., began to encourage him to join Pine Valley, but it took until 1957 for Bill to add this membership to the one at Philadelphia Country Club. He had resigned from Plainfield Country Club because no non-resident membership was available but rejoined Plainfield when it offered the limited option.

"Little did I know," said Bill about joining Pine Valley, "how famous and revered it would become." As the club's fame spread, friends of Bill began asking about playing there, and in September 1958, he took three guests who would form the foundation of something special. They were Joe Hagerty from Villanova and Penn Law School; Lou Merlini from Villanova, who also would have 15 children; and Frank Marshall from Penn State and Penn Law School, who would have 11 children.

They enjoyed the outing so much that they agreed to do it again in 1959, adding a second foursome of Ed McGoldrick, a member of Whitemarsh Valley Country Club and a friend of Hagerty's; John Mezzanotte from Whitemarsh Valley, Villanova and Penn Medical School; Sid Duke from Whitemarsh Valley; and Al Aspen, a friend of Bill's from Philadelphia Country Club.

The same eight golfers returned in 1960 and 1961. In 1962, another foursome joined them: John Aspen, Al's brother; Jake Moran from Villanova, Whitemarsh Valley and, later, Philadelphia Country Club; Frank Queally, a fellow Equitable manager from New York, who belonged to the renowned Winged Foot Golf Club; and Duke Steimling, a friend of the Aspens.

Frank Marshall referred to the gathering as the Pine Valley Open, but Bill felt the club would not lend its name to an event it did not control, so it became the Walsh Open with Pine Valley's concurrence. As time went on, the number of participants steadily increased, and it became more organized, with a trophy for the annual winner and a large permanent platter with the winner's name inscribed each year. Eventually, Bill presented small silver plates to each player each year.

A Callaway scoring system, allowing the deduction of scores on certain holes, was used to determine the winner. "Over the years," Bill said, "this format has worked very well, and all levels of golfers have won the tournament. Though better golfers have won more often than those with higher handicaps, I am still convinced it is the best way to run a tournament for golfers of varying ability."

When the group swelled to 32 golfers, the Walsh Open was pushed back in the fall to avoid using the course at a popular time for members. It took place thereafter on November 15 or the following Tuesday if November 15 fell on a Saturday, Sunday or Monday.

"Though we had about a half-dozen really bad, cold, rainy days and even snow on one occasion," Bill pointed out, "most of the weather was surprisingly good. The tournament was never postponed. Rain or shine, we persevered."

When the group expanded to 40, Bill needed to involve an additional Pine Valley member for each seven guests, but he said, "I was able to do this without too much trouble. The members enjoyed participating in the tournament and the camaraderie following the golf."

The most frequent winner of the Walsh Open, Ray Marchuk, came from Metuchen, New Jersey, Bill's former hometown. He is a close friend of Bill's brother David. Joe Moran from Overbrook Golf Club took the top prize seven times, one less than Marchuk.

Bill decided that the 50th Walsh Open on November 15, 2007, was a fitting time to conclude the event. Pine Valley permitted 48 participants that day, and Bill was able to invite his sons to take part. One of them, Tim, was the winner with a gross score of 81 and a Callaway score of 70.5. "There was much celebration that afternoon and a certain amount of sadness that all this was going to end, but I felt that after so many years, it was the right time to end it."

Ray Marchuk took photos at the final Walsh Open, and Bill received a framed photo collage with signatures and comments from each participant. "It was an extremely thoughtful thing for Ray to do," Bill noted. "I appreciated it so much that it is hanging in the most prominent place in my office. With 225 people playing in the Walsh Open over the 50 years of its existence, those who repeatedly participated became good friends, and a large percentage became policyholders of mine. It was nice to have everything work out so well."

Pine Valley's fame attracts golfers from all over the world, and Bill has played with some prominent visitors. Troy Aikman, when he was in his prime as the Dallas Cowboys' quarterback, was invited to the club by a friend of Bill's from Equitable. "He was taller than I was, six-foot-five, and a strong-looking man," Bill remembers. "He used no more than a 3-iron on any tee but was straight with it and shot an 83, seldom being in trouble."

Jim McMahon, the Philadelphia Eagles' quarterback later in his career, used a driver most of the time. "He was spraying his drives all over the place, shooting 89, a very high score for a player with a six handicap," Bill said. "He learned the hard way and was very frank about it after the round, saying, 'I guess you shouldn't hit a driver on this course.' I won quite a bit of money from him that day, but he was very gracious about it as we had lunch."

Bill also played with Brent Musburger, the sports broadcaster. "He also surprised me with how tall he was. I guess he just looked small standing with various NBA Players he was interviewing after games. He shot 93 and was a very friendly person."

Pine Valley is secluded in the strongest sense of the word. It has held only two national competitions in its more than a century of operation—the 1936 and 1985 Walker Cups. Spectator room is limited, and the club goes to great lengths to protect its privacy. It is open to visitors one day a year in late September, the final day of its annual invitational tournament, the Crump Cup, named for the founder. Leading mid-amateur golfers (age 30 and over) and senior amateurs (age 55 and over) come from all over the United States, Canada and beyond to compete.

Bill's son Chet won the Crump Cup in 1995. Bill qualified for the championship flight three times, advanced to the second flight semi-final once and won the third flight twice.

When Bill reached 50 years of membership at Pine Valley, he qualified for a lifetime free membership. "This is a wonderful gesture and deeply appreciated by those of us who have received it. I wish more clubs had the same practice. I feel extremely fortunate that I was sponsored for membership at Pine Valley and thank Mel Dickenson Jr. deeply."

Matt shared fond memories of a rainy day at Pine Valley in 1971. Bill invited him and Michael, provided they got their 1970s-style hair cut. Michael rebelled, so Bill and Matt played as a twosome. On the 12th tee, two golfers who would become fairly famous caught up with them—Ben

Crenshaw and Tom Kite. They were in the region for the U.S. Amateur Championship at Wilmington Country Club and were rained out at that course so they accepted an invitation to play at Pine Valley. They played two holes with Bill and Matt before moving on. Matt wondered, "Why did I have to get a haircut to play at Pine Valley if Ben Crenshaw can be walking around with his Prince Valiant hairdo?"

"Matt, when you become as good a golfer as Ben Crenshaw, you won't have to get your hair cut, either," Bill told him.

Matt's brother Brendan idolized Crenshaw and sent him a letter inviting him to stay with the Walshes when he came to the 1981 U.S. Open at Merion. Crenshaw did not accept the offer, but Brendan had considerable contact with him as head professional at The Country Club when the Ryder Cup took place there in 1999. Crenshaw captained the victorious United States team.

Bill bothered his friend Stan Engle by insisting on handling all the details at the Walsh Open. "I played in the Walsh Open for many years," Stan remembers. "I was always so frustrated. Bill would do all that paperwork. When everybody came in, he's tallying up everything, and he's handing out the drink tickets. I'm trying to say, 'If we can get this thing on the computer, we can do so much better.' So finally, I persuaded him to let me be his 'secretary,' and I would get down there early and get everybody registered, and they'd pick their score, and draw for their partner, and I'd give them their drink tickets, just so that Bill could perhaps enjoy himself a little bit more rather than having to run around and do all that stuff, run out and play golf, and then come back in and do all his bets. God forbid somebody else doing his bets for him. But the point is not what I did but the kind of guy Bill is, that he just wanted to do everything. He wanted his guests and his associates and friends to be relaxed, not have any responsibilities and just enjoy themselves."

Another friend of Bill's, Mike Greenberg, entertained Bill for golf soon after they met, and Bill typically wanted to reciprocate. He left a message with Mike's wife, Peggy, asking if he could fill an opening in an outing at Pine Valley. Mike found a chance to play at fabled Pine Valley so hard to believe that he accused his wife of playing a joke on him. "No," she said, "I wrote it down." Mike called Bill, and sure enough, he was in the Walsh Open, and he stayed on the invitation list through the 50th anniversary.

Walsh Open trophy winners and participants appear as appendices.

CHAPTER 24

Golfing in Florida

Bill's and Barbara's exposure to Florida during agency managers' meetings convinced them to spend the cold-weather months in the Sunshine State. They rent in Tequesta from early January into May. Both enjoyed golf at the Jupiter Hills Club for many years; today Bill plays at Tequesta Country Club, while Barbara frequents the bridge tables at Jupiter Hills, where they often dine with friends.

Bill earlier was approached about joining Seminole Golf Club, whose course, designed by Donald Ross, is rated among the best in the United States. The application process there went on for several years, and meanwhile, two friends from the Philadelphia area suggested Bill join them at Jupiter Hills, which had just opened with a course designed by George Fazio from Philadelphia. Helping to build that course was George's nephew Tom, who became one of the best-known golf architects in the world.

Bill really liked the Seminole course, but the Jupiter Hills course also was appealing, and Barbara questioned whether they would be comfortable at Seminole, considered a rather stodgy club for older people. They decided Jupiter Hills would be the best place for them, and since Bill knew George Fazio and the club manager, Howard Everitt, also from Philadelphia, the approval process went quickly.

Bill's new home course in Florida, Tequesta, was designed by Dick Wilson, a top architect with courses such as Laurel Valley and Radnor Valley to his credit.

Golfers will appreciate knowing that the first professional at Tequesta was Dow Finsterwald, long a leading player on the PGA Tour who won the national PGA Championship in 1958 at Llanerch Country Club near Philadelphia, the first year it was contested at stroke play.

CHAPTER 25

Special Mother's Day Gift

Barbara knew she was marrying a golfer but confesses she began to resent all the time Bill spent on the golf course. "Then," she recalls, "he brought clubs home for me one Mother's Day. I was just so glad that I learned to play. We played together, not all the time, but we were pretty successful as a team in some of those alternate-shot tournaments. Golf has been a big part of my life. My best friends I've met through golf. It was Bill bringing those clubs home that really made a difference."

Barbara has made her own distinctive mark as a golfer and a leader of golf organizations. She started as a substitute on the women's fifth team at Philadelphia Country Club and advanced through every team to play for the first team when it won the Philadelphia Cup in 1979. In addition to playing with Bill in team events, she partnered with various sons and daughter Tez in competitions.

She ran the club junior program for several years and served as junior chairman and secretary for the Women's Golf Association of Philadelphia. She was a member of the Pennsylvania State Women's Golf Committee and a trustee of the J. Wood Platt Caddie Scholarship Trust. She served for 21 years on the committee that ran her close friend Helen Sigel Wilson's Ladies Leukemia golf tournament.

Unfortunately, numerous operations for joint replacements eventually kept her off the golf course.

"I loved golf," Barbara emphasizes. "It gave me a sense of contributing something and making a difference. It made me think that I could be something other than just a mother. I think people respected me."

Barbara's lowest handicap was 16 and her lowest score 78 at the Skytop Resort. She made three holes-in-one, two at Philadelphia Country Club and one at the PGA Course in Palm Beach Gardens, Florida.

Bill recalls her ace on Philadelphia Country's fifth hole, a downhill par 3 with a pond in front of the green, a stream running along the right side and a large tree left of the green, which is also protected by two large sand bunkers. It's a formidable challenge just to put the tee shot on the green. Barbara called Bill at the office to tell him about the hole-in-one, and he said, "What did you do, hit a tree or something?" She replied, "As a matter of fact, yes. The ball hit that big tree and bounced over that front bunker and went right in the hole." For the memorable shot, she used a 4-wood loaned to her by Herbie Ashburn, the wife of Richie Ashburn, the Hall of Fame baseball player.

"Barbara was one happy woman," Bill noted, "and we had an extra dinner out that week. She made great progress since I bought clubs for her for Mother's Day in 1958, and it added even more happiness to our marriage."

CHAPTER 26

Gentlemen in Red Blazers

B ill has been a leader and successful participant in the Philadelphia
Seniors' Golf Association for the past 30 years. When the family
moved to Philadelphia in 1955, he began to notice results of the group's
tournaments in the *Philadelphia Inquirer*. Possible involvement was a long
way off since members had to be at least 55 years old, but when he reached
that age, Bill was invited to join by Harry Radcliffe, a fellow member at
Philadelphia Country Club, and he was accepted in 1981.

The group, which is not affiliated with the Golf Association of
Philadelphia, began in 1920, according to early minutes, as a "banding
together of men 55 and over who could play a friendly game of golf and dine
and sing the old songs together at various clubs." That concept continues
today as the members, always clad in red blazers and ties, conclude their
outings by singing the old songs.

Bill Ogren of St. Davids Golf Club, a recent president of the
organization, explains: "This is a unique group of people. Almost invariably
they have been prominent and successful in their life endeavors. Many
friendships have developed. It's much more than a golf organization."

The association conducts eight outings each season, six at Golf
Association of Philadelphia clubs and two on the road, usually at the Jersey

Shore and the Poconos. Although the association is not affiliated with GAP, members must belong to a GAP club. The trips to resorts normally last three days, and many wives participate in the golf. Membership is limited to 165 golfers, no more than 16 from a club.

Prizes are awarded to individuals and teams of four players. Winners normally receive a sleeve of three Titleist golf balls, although there are individual trophies for a few special tournaments.

"When I first joined," Bill remembers, "my name appeared a lot in the *Inquirer* as the low-gross winner. By my count, I finished first for low gross 49 times, but my name hasn't appeared in the *Inquirer* in a long time. Each year younger golfers come in, and they are usually the winners. That's what keeps the organization so vibrant and so popular among 55-and-over golfers."

Tournaments normally start with continental breakfast or lunch, followed by golf, cocktails and dinner, finishing early enough so members do not have to drive home in the dark.

Bill advanced through the association offices, serving as president for two years in the late 1980s. "I have gotten to know many fine gentlemen in the organization, some of whom have become very good friends. I still look forward to the tournaments, even though I have little or no chance of winning. For an organization founded in 1920, it is remarkable that it is still around and is so well managed. I strongly recommend it."

CHAPTER 27

Adventures in Ireland

Fifteen years after his golfing trip to Scotland, Bill went to Ireland in September 1995, this time with six of his sons and a friend, Stan Engle, who replaced one son who could not attend. Son, Tim, made the arrangements, starting with a limousine ride to John F. Kennedy International Airport in New York and an overnight flight to Dublin.

Bill tells how the trip proceeded:

Though it was difficult to get much sleep, we somehow were able to arrive at dawn, eat breakfast, settle down in our quarters—a nice bed and breakfast run by a ruddy-faced Irish woman who was most gracious and accommodating—and play the Island Club that morning.

It was very close to where we were staying, and our two rental vans got us there for our 11 a.m. starting time. Though nobody played too well (we were still so tired, I guess), we did enjoy the course and felt that it was a good course to play first as it was less difficult than most of the rest of the courses probably would be.

The next morning we had an early tee time at Portmarnock, a famous Irish layout that had hosted many important tournaments, including the Walker Cup (the United States vs. the British Isles). It was so windy and so cold that no one played well. I can remember I had a 92, which even in those days was not good. Chet and Tim shot 78 and 81, respectively.

By early afternoon the wind had lessened considerably, and the sun was out, so the conditions were much better. We teed off at Royal Dublin, more famous for its "Royal" designation by a former king or queen, than the caliber of the golf course, but it was still an enjoyable test of golf, and the members there were very kind to us—buying us drinks, etc. This was not what we experienced at the first two clubs, where we were buying the Irish drinks, something it appeared they not only welcomed but expected.

County Louth was another fine golf course we played the next day, though not as heralded as Portmarnock or some other courses we would play. The greens, we all agreed, were the best we experienced in Ireland.

On the next day, we played Ardglass, a short course with lots of water. Because of Mass in the morning, we played at 2 p.m. and enjoyed it very much, all having good scores.

On our next stop, we tackled what in the opinion of most of us was the best course we played, Royal County Down, a beautiful course ranked among the top 10 in the world. We were so happy we played this gem that we felt it would be a mistake not to play it again, so we talked the club into letting us play a second round that afternoon, and we were even more pleased.

After this wonderful day, we played another great layout up in the northern tip of Ireland, Royal Portrush, usually ranked in the top 15 in the world. Though it was no doubt a great golf course, it rained hard the entire day, and while we kept playing, we never could fully appreciate the spectacular layout it is reputed to be.

We had a very nice dinner at the club that evening, arranged by one of the members we had met, and went back for a good night's rest before leaving the next morning for the southwestern part of Ireland, where we were to play Rosses Point (also called Sligo). The trip was without mishap, and although there was plenty of wind, the rain had stopped, so it was a relief. We didn't want to have to play any more in the heavy rain with umbrellas blowing inside out. While Rosses Point was a fine golf course and very enjoyable to play, it was not on a level with Royal County Down and Royal Portrush.

The next morning, we left early to arrive in time to play another fairly famous Irish golf course, Tralee. We enjoyed it, though it was fairly windy.

The long-awaited final test for us to experience the next day was one of the most renowned Irish links courses, Ballybunion, which boasts two beautiful courses—the Old and the New. The Old, which we played, is the better known. Though very windy (Ireland seems to be famous for that), the temperature was in the 60s, and for Ireland, very comfortable. We wore "long johns" most of the time on this trip.

We pretty much agreed that Ballybunion should be ranked second behind Royal County Down but ahead of Royal Portrush and Portmarnock. We had dinner in the Ballybunion clubhouse that evening and then went back to our B&B to pack up and get ready to go home.

We all thanked Tim for his planning and arrangements and talked about wanting to go back to Ireland sometime in the future.

Our wives were very happy to see us, and they also appeared to be very happy hearing that we had such an enjoyable time.

It didn't take Bill long to learn that his seven sons were planning another golfing trip to Ireland for the summer of 1997 as a treat in honor of his 75th birthday. While the birthday was actually on March 23, the trip was scheduled in September in hopes of favorable weather. Bill suggested spending the entire trip in southwestern Ireland to reduce the time driving between locations. With Tim again making the arrangements, they flew to Shannon Airport, rather than Dublin.

Bill recounts how the trip went:

We had a smooth flight, and although we were tired again after traveling at night, that afternoon we played the New Course at Ballybunion, which we had not played in 1995. The course was beautiful, the weather, except for a 10-minute shower, was very good, and we all had a very enjoyable afternoon and dinner that evening.

The following morning we went over to Tralee, where we had been two years before, and enjoyed another day of windy golf in Ireland.

We did double duty on the following day, playing two courses in Killarney—Killeen in the morning and Mahony's in the afternoon. While slightly inferior to most of the courses we had played previously, they were very pretty and featured quite a few water hazards. They seemed more like U.S. courses.

One of the more famous Irish courses we didn't get to play in 1995 was Waterville, a very different and beautiful seaside course in the extreme southwest of Ireland. It is ranked in the top 10 courses in Great Britain and is very popular with American visitors. Jerry O'Grady, his wife, Kay, and children, are good friends of ours at Philadelphia Country Club. Jerry had an uncle who lived part-time in Ireland. He was a member of Waterville, and the 17th hole is named in his honor. Waterville is beautiful and is an excellent golf course. We liked it so much that we played twice.

The caddies in Ireland are a story in themselves. I had a nice man about 25 years old the first morning—a fine caddie, except that he wore a green shirt that smelled. We talked about him that night at dinner. Lo and behold, two days later, I had the same caddie, same green shirt and an even stronger aroma about him.

We had a nice lunch at Waterville both days. The weather there was the warmest we experienced during either Ireland trip.

We next played Adare Manor, like both Killarney courses a parkland style with no links features. It is very beautiful and pretty difficult. It also had rained hard here, and the fairways were very soggy, quite rare in the British Isles.

After our first Waterville round, we played a short course nearby called Dooks. We all thought we'd tear the course apart, but it handled us, except for Chet and Brendan, who were able to put enough spin on the ball. The holes were not long, but the greens were very well bunkered, and their surfaces were like concrete. I kept bouncing over them with what I felt were good shots. Then the shot back would be even more difficult to stop. I shot my highest Ireland score there—93.

We played again at Rosses Point (Sligo) in the afternoon after

experiencing another course in the morning that was new to us—
Enniscrone, after which a relatively new course in Chester County,
Pennsylvania, Inniscrone, was named.

Both Enniscrone and another course that was new to us, Connemara,
were good, fairly difficult courses but didn't make the top of our list. One
that we did play again and was still in the top three was the Old (Cashen)
Course at Ballybunion, a truly great links layout. Though it was quite
windy, Buck, our youngest son, and one who never took golf too seriously,
shot 39 on the back nine and won $10 from me—which I heard about for
the next three or four years. He was one happy kid, as he also won money
from most of the others, who usually beat him quite handily. It was good
to see Buck in the limelight; his work schedule in London prevented him
from spending much time playing golf.

We celebrated with dinner that night in the Ballybunion dining room,
partly to talk about Buck's 39 and also because five of our group were
leaving the next day. During dinner, an Irish couple passed our table
and saw all the boys with similar looks. The woman asked, "Are you all
brothers?" They answered, "Yes." She then asked, "Do you have any sisters?"
Again a "Yes, eight of them." She then looked toward me and asked, "Is
that your father?" Again a "Yes." She said, "My God, he must be a sex
maniac." We laughed about that for quite a while. It was a memorable way
to end the day. For the five who had to leave, it was another very enjoyable
Ireland golfing vacation we would cherish for the rest of our lives.

Tim and I were leaving a day later, so we were able to play at Lahinch
that afternoon. This is a notable course in southwestern Ireland. It is on the
sea, is windy most of the time and is most famous for having a completely
blind hole. There is a small mountain in front of you as you stand on the
tee. You really don't know where you should aim, except for a relatively
small white boulder in the middle of the top of the mountain. The hole's
length is about 160 yards, but usually there is a strong wind partly against
you so it plays longer. The other hazard we faced that day was heavy rain for
roughly 10 minutes of every hour, but Tim and I enjoyed the experience.

We had dinner together that night and left from Shannon Airport the
next morning after discussing at length what a wonderful time we had.

At my age, and with the increasingly busy schedules of each of our sons, I don't know whether there will be another golfing trip like this one and the one in 1995, but I will always remember both of them with much fondness.

CHAPTER 28

50,000 Golf Balls and Counting

Bill Walsh is an elusive golfer. On the golf course, he's often hard to find. While his playing partners stroll the fairways, Bill often disappears into the woods or tall grass, summoned by the siren call of lost golf balls.

Bill's friend, Ken Warren, says of playing at Pine Valley, "You're walking to your tee shots, and all of a sudden, Bill's not next to you. He's in the woods. He would find golf balls all over the place. He always knew where the good places to look were."

It is fair to call Bill's search for golf balls an obsession. Not only does he conduct his quest during rounds, but he wanders amidst trees and undergrowth Sunday evenings at Philadelphia Country Club after most of the golfers have gone home.

As with other aspects of his life, Bill's golf ball hobby is highly organized. Starting in the late 1980s, he began keeping track of how many he found, trying to set a new record each year. In the 1990s, he usually found at least 2,500 balls a year.

The total grew to 3,230 in 2002, 3,860 in 2005 and 4,114 in 2007 before the economic slowdown hit. Fewer golfers meant fewer lost balls, and Bill's total dropped to just over 3,200 in 2008 and 2009, to 2,033 in

2010 and to 1,901 in 2011, a year when rainy weather kept golfers off the course.

The search has an unselfish motive since Bill covets golf balls not to use them himself but to give them away. He spends countless hours washing them in laundry soap and bleach, organizing them and putting them in manufacturers' boxes that are saved for him by friends and employees at golf clubs. Outings at Philadelphia Country Club have been another source of empty boxes, since the sponsors usually gave each participant new golf balls.

Bill sorts the balls not only by brand but by specifics within a brand. He arranges Titleists, for example, by Pro-V-1, Pro-V-1x, NXT, SoLo, etc. Twelve balls fit in a box, and Bill gives two or three dozen during the holiday season to friends and relatives. He holds "Golf Ball Day" in late December for those attending the 6:30 a.m. Mass at Our Mother of Good Counsel Church, giving away bags of loose golf balls in the church parking lot.

Bill acknowledges that he draws some stares while he searches: "I'm sure the people who see me at Philadelphia Country Club every Sunday night looking for golf balls wonder if I'm some kind of nut, but they all seem to accept me as I am and ask how many I've found that day. I stay out of their way and most of all, know enough about golfing manners that I don't distract them in any way."

Until recently, Bill could run in the evening and find golf balls at the Jupiter Hills course in Florida when he and Barbara belonged there. Now friends at the club find balls and save them for him.

One of his friends at Jupiter Hills, Stafford Gellatly, tried to do Bill a favor a few years ago when he rummaged through his house and found about 400 old golf balls. He packed them up and put them at the end of his driveway for Bill to pick up, but a workman thought they were trash and carted them away. Bill chased after the truck to no avail.

"Barbara thinks I'm a little kooky," Bill admits, "for letting Golf Ball Sunday be such a big part of my summer and fall life, but I keep doing it. You'd be surprised how much people appreciate those free golf balls, all polished and ready for play and, in most cases, in their proper boxes."

Which balls does Bill find most often? Titleist ProV-1 is the most popular, with 20 percent of the total, followed by Titleist ProV-1x at 12 percent, other Titleists at 11 percent, Callaway at 10 percent, Nike and Spalding Top Flite at eight percent each, and a combination of 15 others totaling 23 percent.

Bill's friend Stan Engle recalls an incident involving Bill's hunger for golf balls at Philadelphia Country Club:

I'm playing Warren Deakins in the senior club championship, and Bill was playing with us, kind of like a monitor. We were on the 17th hole, and the match was very close. From the tee, you walk across a dam and then up a hill. There are a lot of woods back there. Bill typically would go over the dam and instead of walking straight up the hill like everybody else, he'd turn right and go through the woods to look for balls.

Deak and I are at the top of the hill. Deak's trying to hit his second shot, and Bill's in the woods rustling around and rustling around and rustling around. Every time Warren tries to hit his shot, he has to back away. He backs away two or three times and finally yells at Bill, "Be quiet." Bill says, "I can't find my driver." He had seen some golf balls and laid his club down to fish for them and then couldn't find his driver. That's why he was making so much noise.

CHAPTER 29

Augusta National – No. 500

When Bill first played golf with his grandfather at Galloping Hill Golf Course, a public club in Kenilworth, New Jersey, that was the only course he knew existed. His next course was Sunnybrook, another public course, and his third was Metuchen Golf and Country Club.

Bill steadily added courses to his repertoire but didn't pay much attention to all the places he played until 1995, when he was having lunch at Jupiter Hills in Florida with Cy Eastlack, a member there and at Pine Valley. He showed Bill a list of the 485 golf courses he had played as he tried to reach 500. Bill borrowed the list, made a copy and started a record of his own, using Cy Eastlack's list as a starting point. Helped by notes he had kept, Bill counted up the courses he had played in college, in tournaments and at hotels and resorts. "My total was an amazing 365," Bill learned. "When I discovered my total was at least 100 more than I thought it would be, I made the decision that I had to get to 500 different courses before I died—another goal in my life. I naturally began to concentrate on the courses that were easy to get to and not too expensive."

John Klotz, a longtime friend from Penn Law School, agreed to join Bill in seeking out courses they had not played, adding one new course a month. They started with the municipal courses in Philadelphia, then spread to the suburbs. "We discovered some very nice layouts," Bill noted, "and we felt that what relatively little we had to spend was well worth it." Bill added more courses to the list as he played in tournaments, member-guests and business outings plus trips to Scotland and Ireland. By the end of 2000, the total stood at 474.

Stan Engle, Bill's friend from Philadelphia Country Club and Jupiter Hills, said to him, "You belong to Pine Valley, you've played most of the top courses in the United States and a few really famous ones in Great Britain. Why don't you try to arrange to play at Augusta National for the 500th course?" Augusta National, home of the Masters Tournament, is one of the top-ranked golf courses in the world, so the suggestion made sense to Bill. "What golfer wouldn't want to play Augusta at any time," he thought, "particularly one in my situation? The catch was to find someone who would be willing to sponsor me there. It was impossible to get on the course otherwise, and the member had to be there when you arrived at the front gate, play the round with you, and after the round, you had to leave the premises when he did."

Bill remembered that his friend Dr. Ken Warren had a friend, Jerry Beasley, from South Carolina, whom Bill had met and who knew a member of Augusta National. He was able to arrange for Bill and Ken to play the Masters course on May 7, 2002.

Bill's course total reached 498 by the end of March, and he held it there, planning to play with Jerry Beasley May 6 at Camden Country Club in South Carolina and the next day at Augusta National.

Unfortunately, about 10 days before the eagerly anticipated date, Bill slipped and fell at home in Florida, breaking his left elbow and sidelining him from golf for several months. His host at Augusta National, Bob Timmerman, agreed to postpone the round there until November 7.

"I didn't start playing golf again, after many days of special exercises, until mid-October. My scores were not very good, but I did have my sixth hole-in-one at Philadelphia Country Club's Centennial Nine fifth hole. After playing four more rounds, I realized I was not yet back to my pre-accident level but was very thankful that I could at least get around the Augusta course."

Bill recounts the memorable day when he finally played Augusta National:

"The entire club and golf course are pristine pure—not a scrap of paper, not an unfilled divot, not a weed, not a blade of grass that should be cut. The clubhouse was old but beautifully kept up and freshly painted. Most of the bunkers are large and filled with the whitest and finest sand. The changes in elevation on the putting surfaces are amazing—over four feet in some instances on the same greens that appear to be almost level when shown on television in the Masters.

"None of us scored well. I started off only two over par for the first five holes but three-putted the next three greens and finished the front nine with 43, the best in the group. However the back nine was a disaster as I had six more three-putt greens and a few water problems, which gave me a horrendous 54 on the back nine for an embarrassing 97. I don't think Augusta is going to invite me to play in the Masters.

"You look back at that day and realize how difficult the greens are, how tough the entire course is, but you nevertheless worship the place and all its beauty. I shall never forget my wonderful day there, and I profusely thank Dr. Ken Warren, Jerry Beasley and Bob Timmerman for putting it all together."

When Bill reached his goal of playing 500 different courses, he decided to keep going and by January 2012, he had increased the total to 600.

The golf courses played by Bill Walsh appear as an appendix.

When Bill reached the age of 65, he began to think about a goal common to golfers—shooting his age, an 18-hole score totaling no more than his age. At age 70, he thought it was possible, and at 72, he shot his age for the first time March 23, 1994, at Jupiter Hills in Florida, repeating his 72 three weeks later.

"They made quite a big thing of this at Jupiter Hills," Bill recalls, "and figured it would become a regular occurrence. This was not to be, however, and I didn't do it again in Florida that year or at Philadelphia Country Club that summer."

That fall Bill played in a Philadelphia Seniors tournament in the Poconos and needed to shoot 75 in the final round to win. He concentrated so hard on posting a winning score that he did not realize he had shot his age, 72, for the third time until his playing partner mentioned it. He failed to increase his total at age 73 but shot his age seven times at 74, eight times at 75 and seven times at 76.

Bill went on to become the first golfer in Philadelphia Country Club history to shoot his age 50 times, and he passed 100 times by the age 85. His elbow injury in 2002 slowed the pace, but the total passed 250 in 2009, and reached 334 by the end of 2011.

CHAPTER 30

The "Raiders" and the "Whites"

Bill's participation in Golf Association of Philadelphia and club championships decreased as he grew older, but his compelling interest in golf did not diminish. He found steady outlets for friendly competition at both Philadelphia Country Club and Tequesta Country Club.

Philadelphia Country brings together golfers over age 65 who play Tuesdays and Thursdays. Bill's friend Jim McLellan started the program in the 1980s. When Bill passed age 65 and could take more time away from the office, he began to participate. Members of "The Raiders" start their rounds between 11 a.m. and noon. Advance commitments are not needed. Pairings are drawn by lot, and starting times are arranged by the caddiemaster, Chris Kopko. The entry fee of $5 goes toward prizes. The winning foursome buys a round of drinks.

"The participants have not only a competitive round of golf with friends," according to Bill, "but an enjoyable social hour afterward. Even those who lost are generally in a good mood when they leave the club to go home. This wonderful idea of Jim McLellan's has grown into a very enjoyable golfing experience for the old codgers who participate, and the handicapping system keeps anyone from gaining a monopoly on the winnings. I have enjoyed the tournaments very much and have developed much stronger friendships with fellows I knew only slightly before. It is a pleasure to be a member of 'The Raiders.' Paul DeLomba has been an efficient leader since Jim McClellan's death."

The group holds an annual cocktail party and dinner at Philadelphia Country Club that includes wives of members and widows of deceased members. A member, Don Smith, who is a photographer, presents a slide show of Raiders on the golf course with shots over water, out of sand bunkers and other humorous situations.

When Bill played at Jupiter Hills in Florida, his companions often were friends from Philadelphia, including Stan Engle, Paul Missett, Jim Yarnall, Craig Ammerman, Joe Mack, Ben Canavan, Cas Holloway, Sam Niness and Jerry O'Grady.

As time went on, his base of playing partners grew to include Dick Curtis, Frank Feroleto, Don Danner, Bill Tuggle, Bernie Deverin, Jack Lynch, Jack Gardner, Staff Gellatly, Jim Dunn, Dr. Frank Gerard, Tom Hudson, Steve Lynch, George Manos, George Stradley and Ben Torcivia.

Once Bill and Barbara transferred to Tequesta, he thought he might have trouble getting games because he did not know many members, but he was pleasantly surprised to learn the club held open tournaments four days a week, teeing off at 10:30 Monday and Wednesday and at 8:30 Friday and Saturday, plus a shotgun tournament Thursday at 1:00 and a Men's Golf Association tournament Tuesday at 8:30, not to mention mixed tournaments every Sunday. "I had never before seen a golf course in Florida with such a friendly arrangement for new members," said Bill. "I have met many really nice people and am having a most enjoyable time there."

The four-day-a-week tournaments offer prizes to teams and for the low net score on holes, funded by $10 entry fees. Those who play with "The Whites" use the white tees, distinguished from "The Blues," who play from the longer blue tees. "The Blues" are mostly younger and better players than "The Whites," so it is appropriate for them to play a tougher course.

Bill pointed out, "As far as old guys like me are concerned, they let us play from special tees that are shorter than the whites, but we have to give up seven strokes of our handicaps. This practice is what the United States Golf Association recommends and is understood by all the competitors."

There is more interest in the results at Tequesta than at Philadelphia Country, Bill noted, because the prize money is twice as much.

"I am really enjoying Tequesta," he said, "not only for the golf but also the many new friends, the courtesy of the staff and the very good meals. We owe special thanks to Jim Curtain for overseeing 'The Whites' tournaments with the help of Tom Coleman, the locker room attendant. They were so gracious and helpful in making me feel very much at home at Tequesta along with the golf pro, Chris Hayes, and his staff and the other employees of this fine club. Following Jim's Death, Chris Bates has ably succeeded him.

"Among the members I have gotten to know pretty well who play in 'The Whites' tournaments are Mike Adams, Hal Alwood, Chris Bates, Al Borup, Dr. Lou Bragaw, Peter Brennan, John Breslin, Bill Collins, Paul Compare, Jim Curtain, Bob Cusmano, Jeff Eyke, Walt Foran, Glen Gerdelmann, Don Johnson, Carl Kapikian, John Korb, Pat Massa, Howard and Rick McKee, Bob Mitscher, Buzz Murphy, Harry Riordan, Frank Ronayne, Charlie Sage, Al Schraifel, Ed Sharbaugh, Fred Smallhoover, Dr. Paul Swade, Don Webster, Dr. Gary Weiss and Dave Williams."

Bill's career in the insurance business reflects numerous
achievements, honors and leadership positions.

During an afternoon break from a business meeting in
Switzerland in April, 1988, Bill and Barbara enjoy the Alps.

The 15 Walsh children helped Bill and Barbara celebrate their 60th wedding anniversary. (Photo by V.I.P. Studios, Inc., Ken Schurman.)

Dan Walsh created this acrylic on canvas, entitled "Notes," in 2010.

As Artist in Residence at the Portland Art Museum, Lexa Walsh gives fun, interpretive tours of the collection.

CHAPTER 31

Business Organizations

B ill Walsh's lofty standing in the insurance business is confirmed by the countless honors and achievements he has attained through the years.

The Old Guard, an organization of Equitable agency managers, selected Bill as the company's 1987 National Honor Agent, the highest tribute an agent can receive from the group. He became the first former Old Guard president to receive the honor. Agency managers formed the Old Guard in 1905 to give them a vehicle to get changes made by the Home Office that agents and district managers felt would improve the company.

The managers hold annual meetings at their own expense at resort hotels. When Bill served as president in 1974, the meeting took place at The Homestead, a highly rated resort in Virginia with three golf courses, including the Cascades, ranked among the top 50 courses in the country.

"Though this meeting was mostly involved with what we were asking for, including possible changes in relationships with the Home Office," Bill explained, "our requests never involved any compensation for the agency managers. We were there for the good of our agents. We invited several officers from the Home Office, including the president. It was a chance for them to get to know us better and vice versa. We agency managers came away from these meetings with the feeling that we had accomplished something, even if it was merely getting to know the top officers of the company better. The Old Guard meetings are still going on today, and even though the Home Office is playing a bigger role than it used to, they are still very important to managers and their agents, and being elected president of the Old Guard is still a coveted role and an important honor in a manager's career."

The Million Dollar Round Table, a status Bill first reached in 1956, previously signified sales of permanent life insurance of more than $1 million in a year. Bill, as a Life Member by qualifying for at least six consecutive years, could attend the annual meetings of the Round Table. "The meetings were excellent," Bill noted. "The additional knowledge they provided was extremely helpful, both motivationally and financially."

A highlight for Bill was traveling to the 1992 annual MDRT meeting in Chicago to watch daughter Stephanie deliver a talk called "The Stress-less Balancing Act."

The meetings take place in cities throughout the United States and Canada and occasionally in Great Britain and Europe. The Round Table's Foundation makes charitable donations to deserving organizations in areas where members practice their profession.

As an Equitable agency manager, Bill earned 14 Presidential Citation Awards and 25 National Leaders Corps qualifications. His other Equitable recognitions include membership in the Hall of Fame, Centurion Award, two Legion of Honor Awards, Superior Achievement Award, Order of Excalibur, Distinguished Service Award and the Ron Stever Humanitarian Award.

Bill also played an active role in local and national insurance-related organizations:

—The Philadelphia Association of Life Underwriters (now the National Association of Insurance and Financial Advisors–Greater Philadelphia) – President.

– The Pennsylvania Life Underwriters (now the National Association of Insurance and Financial Advisors–Pennsylvania).

– National Association of Life Underwriters (now the National Association of Insurance and Financial Advisors–NAIFA).

These associations function with separate offices and directors, and the state and local groups have representatives on national and state committees. "These organizations work extremely well and are quite powerful politically in Harrisburg, Pennsylvania's capital, and even more so on the national scene in Washington," Bill pointed out.

– American Society of Chartered Life Underwriters–Philadelphia Chapter (now Society of Financial Service Professionals–Greater Philadelphia Chapter) – President.

This organization evolved from the classes and courses sponsored by The American College, which is covered elsewhere in this book. SFSP is the standard-bearer for professionalism and ethical guidance for top advisors. Members have earned recognized professional credentials and assist clients in reaching future financial goals. They make a strong commitment to ethical business practices and continuing education. The Society has its own officers and directors, with chapters throughout the United States and an annual business meeting. The national FSP organization is financially independent of NAIFA, although many agents are active in both it and The American College.

Bill cited Paul Mills and John Driskell as managing directors who did an outstanding job of running the Society, adding that when Driskell retired in 2002, his successor was Joe Frack, "who continues John's excellent performance but under more difficult conditions—The American College trustees decided to sever itself from the Society, much to the chagrin of many CLUs."

– Philadelphia Estate Planning Council – President

Insurance agents and financial advisors number about 25 percent of the members of this organization. Bankers, attorneys and CPAs make up the majority of the membership. The council draws important speakers from throughout the country for meetings at the prestigious Union League in Philadelphia.

When Bill joined the organization in 1955, its golf tournament attracted about two-thirds of the 250 members. Bill looked forward to it, especially because he won the trophy for low-gross score the first few times he played. The outing dropped in popularity for a while, but participation has increased in the last decade.

Bill went through the leadership chairs of the council and served as host for the National Estate Planning meeting in Philadelphia in 1987. "This organization has been very well run for a long time," he said, "largely due to its meeting site and its administrative secretaries—Charlie Merz, Carl Oxholm and June Neff. Though I do not attend as many of the meetings as I used to because of time in Florida, I do still very much admire the organization and the caliber of its officers and directors, and I will continue to be a member."

– General Agents and Managers Conference – Greater Philadelphia – President

This relatively small organization is limited to sales management leaders of life insurance companies. It was quite active in the 1960s and 1970s, and a few Philadelphians went on to become national presidents, a high honor among those in agency management. Bill went through the office chairs and attended a few national meetings.

"Our membership made us respect each other," Bill said, "and we had none of the currently prevalent practice of stealing agents from competitors. I salute fellow members John Cronin, Maurice Stewart, Bob DeCoursey, Dick Tracy, Paul Shevlin, Carl Oxholm, Joe Patton, Frank Bockius and John Knipp for being true gentlemen."

As an Equitable manager, Bill recruited and developed many agents who went on to success in the insurance business. One of them, Paul Missett, not only worked with Bill but became a family friend and golfing partner. They met at Philadelphia Country Club, and Bill convinced Paul to apply at Equitable. Paul was only 23 years old, and the Home Office needed some convincing from Bill that he would make a successful agent. His long career with Equitable certainly justified Bill's faith in him.

"Bill was like a second father to me," Paul commented, "and he has been a dear friend. I consider him my mentor in life. My wife, Celeste, and I owe a lot to Bill and Barbara. They've been a great influence on our lives. Bill is a great father, a great Catholic and Christian, a dedicated family man, someone who loves his business. He is extremely moral in his work and ethics, and he is a very dedicated and focused individual."

Paul praised Barbara's "calmness and serenity in dealing with life and situations, be it health issues or family matters." He added. "She's just a very elegant, classy, wonderful woman with a great equanimity. She's wonderful for Bill, and she's a great influence on everybody who knows her."

Two other outstanding young people Bill recruited were Al Giagnacova (right out of Villanova), who became a very successful agent, and Bob Jones, a graduate of Gettysburg College, who later became agency manager in Pittsburgh and eventually a senior vice president in Equitable's home office.

Though Al and Bob, and their wives, Luci and Sharon, respectively, live with their children outside of the Philadelphia area, they and the Walshes remain good friends.

CHAPTER 32

The American College

T he mission of *The American College is to raise the level of professionalism of its students and, by extension, the financial services industry as a whole. By imparting expert knowledge—and by emphasizing that such knowledge must be regularly renewed and ethically applied—The College seeks to strengthen not only its students' professionalism, but also the financial security of individuals, families, businesses, and the societies they serve.*

The American College has been located in the Philadelphia area since its founding in 1927. Bill Walsh received the college's Chartered Life Underwriter degree in 1953 and later became an advocate and staunch supporter.

In 1956, after the Walsh family had moved to St. Davids in the Philadelphia suburbs, Bill was surprised to learn from a neighbor that the college was interested in buying a house across the street from him for its headquarters. This upset the neighbors, who planned to protest at a town meeting.

"Understandably," Bill said, "I was shocked at the news, agreed with the traffic problem it would cause and couldn't understand why the college hadn't informed me about it. While admittedly I was a newcomer to the

Philadelphia area and not too prominent in industry circles yet, I wondered if maybe the college didn't want me to know about it."

Bill told his neighbor, "Look, I'm in a predicament in which I can't go to the meeting and argue against the proposed purchase. I agree not to do anything that would hurt you or your neighbors' position, and if the college people call me, I'll tell them that I don't think it would be the right place for the college. The property is too small with no room for expansion, and it would cause all sorts of traffic problems." The neighbor called Bill to tell him the college plan had been turned down and thanked him for not promoting the purchase.

"I felt relieved," Bill remembers, "that a potentially serious problem had been eliminated and considered the matter closed. Such was not to be." A few months later, a trustee of the college sharply attacked Bill, claiming he was the reason the college plan failed. Bill explained that he was not involved, but the man was not mollified and apparently complained to Dave Gregg, the college president. However, Bill met with Gregg to explain what actually happened. They became close friends, and Bill went on to raise substantial funds for the college. When the Equitable Home Office arranged a television presentation for Bill's National Honor Agent Award at the Old Guard meeting in 1987, Gregg was one of those congratulating Bill. A few years after the St. Davids property plan was rejected, the college bought a large estate in suburban Bryn Mawr. Later it faced some challenges that tested Sam Weese, a former insurance commissioner for the state of West Virginia, who served 15 years as college president.

"He had a lot of critical decisions that had to be made, and he handled them very well," Bill noted. "He made important changes and all in all did a very intelligent job in a most professional way. The college was now being led by a man who knew where he was going and how to get there. The ship had been righted. Though it was unfortunate that he had to convince some longtime employees to take early retirement, he replaced them with individuals with excellent backgrounds who, in all fairness, achieved considerably more than their predecessors."

One of the new employees was Stephen Tarr, an agency head for Farm Family Insurance, who became vice president of development. "Steve did an outstanding job right from the beginning and continues in that capacity today," Bill said. "He and his wife, Alice, have become close friends of Barbara's and mine."

In 2003, Sam Weese was selected to receive the President's Cup Award from the National Association of Insurance and Financial Advisors Greater Philadelphia Chapter, and Bill was honored that the recipient asked him to present the award. After Weese's retirement that same year, his alma mater, West Virginia University, created an endowed professorship in the name of Samuel J. Weese.

Dr. Laurence Barton then became the eighth president of The American College. He had been president of Heald College and DeVry University.

His assessment of the college's status on its large Bryn Mawr campus led him to conclude that most of the acreage should be sold, keeping only one building, since modern educational methods required less classroom space.

"The reaction to this sudden decision," Bill said, "caused more furor than anything ever experienced by the college. Most of the buildings had been largely paid for by contributions from the many former students. A number of large life insurance companies also made annual contributions. Even I, as loyal as I was to the college, couldn't understand how the trustees, many of whom I knew, could go along with such a decision.

"After things had calmed down a little, I began to feel particularly sorry for those individuals who had contributed in extremely large amounts and had their names on rooms and facilities in those buildings that were scheduled to be sold. Some parts of the buildings were dedicated to large givers or members of their families. This action was certainly something that Dave Gregg or Sam Weese would never have taken.

"After about two months," Bill continued, "I finally realized that probably Larry, because he was not a graduate of The American College, did not have the same blind loyalty that we had to our beautiful campus to which we all had contributed. It seemed possible that after a few years, we loyalists would realize that with most of the education now being administered through e-mails, DVDs, etc., using the property's sale to modernize the electronic system of the college so that more students could be attracted to the college might well prove to be, in hindsight, a very wise business decision. Only time will tell. For the good of the college, I just hope that I'm right.

"Now that a few years have gone by and the problems in the world economy have increased dramatically," Bill reflected, "it appears that Larry is a genius for having sold the mortgaged property at such a good price."

The American College honors those whose role in the development of the institution was of special significance with the Huebner Gold Medal, named for the college's founder, Solomon Huebner. It is awarded to individuals who through support and dedication to the college and its programs have moved the institution forward in its mission.

Bill Walsh received the Huebner Gold Medal in 2002. "Very few people have ever received this award," according to Bill's friend Stephen Tarr, the college vice president for development, "and the college has over 150,000 graduates. It is the highest recognition anyone can receive from The American College. I was very proud he received that, and it just indicates the kind of appreciation The American College has for Bill Walsh and his family. I just think he epitomizes what the college would recognize as the person who has earned our designation, and the same goes for his daughter Stephanie and his son Matt, who are involved in the business. To me, Bill is a life insurance agent's life insurance agent. If I was in the insurance business and I needed a life insurance agent, he would be the one that I would want to be my agent. Bill takes care of his clients like no other producer that I know."

Sam Weese, the retired college president, also has high praise for Bill: "He was always willing to help, going the extra mile. Bill was so dependable. If you asked Bill to do something, you never had to ask him twice. He would do it and never ask for anything in return. He was very modest about what he did, and he certainly didn't have to have publicity. He did it because he thought it was the right thing to do.

"So many individuals in the life insurance business have a stereotyped image in that they're very extroverted, they're very much the center of attention when they walk into a room. Bill proved that you don't have to have that kind of personality to be successful. There are ways of communicating and being persuasive that really are more low-key, more based on sincerity, knowledge and credibility. I always admired Bill's success and the way he went about it."

CHAPTER 33

The J. Wood Platt Trust

As Bill was able to spend less time on the insurance business, he became active in the Golf Association of Philadelphia, holding leadership positions and encouraging support of the J. Wood Platt Caddie Scholarship Trust. The Platt Trust provides scholarships to eligible caddies at clubs belonging to GAP. Created in 1958, it awarded $15.1 million to 3,250 students through 2011. Donations from GAP clubs provide most of the funding. Bill has been in charge of soliciting donations from Philadelphia Country Club members, and the club has been the leading contributor for nine of the last 10 years.

As the annual deadline for donations approaches, Bill is a familiar sight at Philadelphia Country, and members find him quite persuasive.

J. Wood "Woody" Platt was a legendary amateur golfer from Philadelphia who also made a mark nationally. He won the Philadelphia Amateur Championship nine times and the GAP Patterson Cup, signifying the stroke-play championship, four times. He won the first United States Golf Association Senior Amateur Championship in 1955. Early in his career, he defeated the fabled U.S. Open champion Francis Ouimet in a U.S. Amateur semifinal match, and he reportedly overcame Bobby Jones in their only two matches against each other.

Woody went on to serve as president of GAP in 1952-53 and 1956. In 1958, Joe Burnett, a close friend of his whose wife, Peg, became executive director of GAP, suggested to Woody the formation of a scholarship fund for caddies. Woody was well known for his generosity to caddies, and the fund was named in his honor when GAP approved the concept, which was advocated by Walter Schmidt, the association president; Leo Fraser, president of the Philadelphia Section of the PGA of America who would become the national president; and Al Keeping, the golf professional at Gulph Mills Golf Club. The J. Wood Platt Caddie Scholarship Trust is operated by GAP. Woody was the first contributor. The modest early fundraising results were encouraging and steadily increased. In the early 1990s with strong backing from Art Kania of Overbrook Golf Club, GAP established a lifetime membership classification costing $10,000, which could be paid over five years. The trust reached the initial goal of 100 members in 2003. As of January, 2012, the membership total was 324.

"Being close to the J. Wood Platt campaign for more than 50 years," Bill pointed out, "I continue to be greatly impressed with the officers and trustees of the Platt Trust and the GAP staff members who have so capably handled the details of the annual fundraising effort and the interviews of the caddies applying for scholarships. Gordon Brewer, Dr. David Junkin and Clark O'Donoghue have done exceptional jobs during their terms as chairmen of the Board of Trustees, and the current chairman, John Endicott, a longtime committee member, is performing the same way. Bob Caucci, who headed the fundraising effort for six years, was very successful. His successor, Barbara Scott, is performing most effectively while getting to know many of the Platt donors.

"Another person who offered his time to the trust for many years was the late Franny Poore, a longtime Philadelphia Country Club member. He did much of the interviewing of scholarship applicants and participated in their selection. The trophy awarded the Outstanding Caddie of the Year bears his name."

Jack Pergolin, a coach of many high school basketball championship teams, has done most of the Caddie Scholarship interviewing since Franny Poore's death. "He has done an excellent job," Bill noted. "Franny would be very proud of him."

At the annual meeting of the Philadelphia Country Club on January 24, 2012, its president, Kevin Rassas, expressed to Bill Walsh the club's gratitude for his many years of service on behalf of the J. Wood Platt Caddie Scholarship Trust. He also presented him with a golf bag. He then gave Bill a framed letter, written to the club, from John Endicott, the chairman of the J. Wood Platt Caddie Scholarship Trust, expressing its gratitude to him for his dedication to the Trust and to the Golf Association of Philadelphia. The letter said:

On behalf of the Trust and its caddie-scholars, we would like to recognize William T. Walsh for his steadfast dedication to the beliefs and ideals of the J. Wood Platt Caddie Scholarship. Under Mr. Walsh's leadership and thanks to the generosity of his fellow members, Philadelphia Country Club has raised a J. Wood Platt all-time high of $1.3 million in donations. Perhaps, most impressively, over the last 10 years, Philadelphia Country Club has donated almost 30 percent more than the next Golf Association of Philadelphia Member Club. With Mr. Walsh representing the Platt and its virtues, Philadelphia Country Club has finished ranked as the No. 1 contributing Golf Association of Philadelphia Member Club in nine of the past 10 years. Philadelphia Country Club also leads in the number of individual contributors, whether it be on the highest level, Lifetime, to introductory Par Club members.

As Bill steps away from his Philadelphia Country Club role as club chairman of the Platt Caddie Scholarship, the entire J. Wood Platt family owes him a great multitude of thanks. Bill's long service to the game on all levels—whether taking one of his 15 children to the course or serving as President of the Golf Association of Philadelphia—Mr. Walsh and his passion have been a beacon for all to admire. In closing, as you step away, Bill, you've definitely embodied J. Wood Platt's mantra to "Give Them All a Chance."

The most famous of the many stories surrounding J. Wood Platt's colorful career involves a round at Pine Valley Golf Club in 1936 with members of the British Walker Cup team. Platt birdied the first hole, eagled the second, scored a hole-in-one on the third and birdied the fourth to go six under par for the first four holes. The fourth green is next to the clubhouse, and the Englishmen were so amazed by Platt's brilliance that they said it called for a drink. A New York sportswriter reported that Woody went to the Pine Valley bar and did not return to the course, saying things couldn't get any better.

Bill tells the outcome differently. As noted earlier, Platt was an Equitable insurance agent when Bill was the agency manager. "One day at lunch," Bill recalls, "I asked Woody about that famous start at Pine Valley and whether he really stopped after the fourth hole. He answered, 'We stopped. The Englishmen were so far down in the match that they suggested stopping, so we each had a couple of drinks, and I went out and finished the round, ending up with a 66. The story about quitting after four holes spread so rapidly that I never bothered to try and refute it. The story was so good that no one would have believed me.' "

Just as Bill Walsh was devoted to Philadelphia Country Club, club members held him in high esteem. In the mid-1990s, they honored him with the naming of the William T. Walsh Stroke Play Championship. Mark Shuman, who with Jim Finegan Jr. suggested the recognition, said, "We wanted to endow the award to insure that the trophy would be maintained in perpetuity and provide a stipend to purchase a small trophy each year to be the permanent property of the winner. We wanted all of this to happen without expense to the club, so I sent out a letter to the male golf membership asking for donations. If my memory serves, I had to send out a second letter telling everyone to stop sending checks because we had received more than enough money. My sense is that I could have raised $100,000 for Bill. Such is the esteem in which Bill is held by all who know him."

CHAPTER 34

A Leading Role with GAP

The Golf Association of Philadelphia, the oldest regional golf association in the United States, began in 1897. Philadelphia Country Club is a founding club. GAP promotes the game of golf, rates courses, provides USGA Handicap Indexes, schedules and regulates tournaments, and provides numerous other services to its 141 member clubs.

Soon after Bill Walsh moved to the Philadelphia area in 1955, he heard about GAP competitions and began to play in some of them, including the Interclub Matches, which involve more than 3,000 golfers from more than 300 teams. Bill recalls, "I was very impressed with the high standard of competition and how capably everything was handled."

In 1991 at the age of 69, Bill won the GAP Senior Amateur Championship, which he considers his most significant golfing achievement. His participation in tournaments put him in contact with fellow competitors and GAP Executive Committee members, leading to an extremely active involvement with the affairs of the association that continues today.

Bill became very close to two GAP leaders, Joe Moran, the past president of the association, and Stan Friedman, the secretary and, for a record 13 years, an Executive Committee member. Another friend in the GAP administration, Franny Poore, frequently competed with Bill in the Philadelphia Country Club championship. His friends suggested Bill would make a good member of the Executive Committee, but he waited until he retired as an Equitable manager before accepting nomination to the committee. He served from 1983 through 1995, including the last three years as president.

Bill received the GAP Distinguished Service Award in 2008 for his contributions to GAP and the betterment of the game of golf. One of his most significant achievements was successfully spearheading a change in the GAP bylaws to permit public golf clubs to belong to the association. Until that vote, only private clubs could belong. "During the 1980s and early 1990s," according to Bill, "there was a quiet but slowly increasing feeling among a few of the Executive Committee members that we should open up the GAP tournaments to non-private clubs. This gained full momentum in my final year as president. Because I felt this was important to the future of GAP and my successor as president was not as enthusiastic as I was, I was asked to stay on the committee for one year and work on getting the bylaws changed. It was a daunting task, as it took a two-thirds favorable vote of the clubs represented at the annual meeting to get the amendment passed."

Bill traveled to GAP clubs to urge support for the bylaws change. "To the credit of all of the members of all of the clubs," he said, "I was never confronted or badgered by any member of any club for putting so much effort in the quest to get the bylaws changed, for which I was very grateful. It was also a good indication of the high type of officers and members of our GAP clubs. Very traditional clubs such as Pine Valley, Merion, Aronimink, Philadelphia Cricket, Saucon Valley, Gulph Mills, Riverton and Philadelphia Country that might have been expected to oppose the change stood squarely in favor of it, helping to pass the amendment, 50 to 10, actually a fairly close margin since 40 favorable votes were needed."

Stan Friedman, who worked with Bill on GAP matters, credits him and Joe Moran for opening GAP to public clubs. Association membership grew significantly. "Bill said the game of golf is played by everybody. Therefore, we cannot be exclusive," Friedman noted. "I've never forgotten those words. That took guts. If I was in the Marines in a war, he could be my platoon leader."

Today, Bill says, "Rightly or wrongly, I still strongly believe that it was the right thing to do and was worth all the effort. One of my greatest boosters was Craig Ammerman, who later became president of the association and was elected to the United States Golf Association Executive Committee. Craig was most outspoken in backing the change, and I thank him for his valiant support as well as the many other Executive Committee members who helped us achieve such a favorable vote.

"Jimmy Sykes, our executive director, was also a 100 percent supporter of the bylaws change right from the beginning and did much to gain approval of the idea. I also greatly appreciate all Jim's help and support during my years on the Executive Committee and particularly during my time as president. I have kept in touch with Jim, and we try to play golf together once a year. When Jim retired, he was succeeded by Mark Peterson, whom he trained. Mark has done an excellent job and has surrounded himself with a very capable staff. The Golf Association of Philadelphia is in good hands."

Bill also developed lasting friendships with Craig Lundberg, a president of GAP, and Arch Waldman, a secretary who was in line to be president before moving to Florida. The three men played golf together frequently in Florida, and their wives became good friends as well. Both Stan Friedman and Arch Waldman passed away in 2011.

CHAPTER 35

Not Cheaper by the Dozen

Feelings from Bill Walsh about the pros
and cons of having so many children:

About the only negative thought I had with so many children was how much it cost, particularly when they started to go to college. The worst time was when we had five in college and two in private Catholic prep school. After lying awake half the night for a week when all the initial tuition payments had to be made, Barbara and I talked about what we should do. She agreed that the best choice was to refinance our mortgage, and that's what we did. Though we hated to do it because it meant a higher interest rate, it was still the best thing we could do at the time, and we never regretted it.

Even with this troubled time, neither of us ever regretted having the children we did—it just awakened us to the cost of having to educate them.

As Barbara and I used to say to each other when we had dinner out just about every Friday night, how grateful we were to have so many wonderful, loving children—not only to the two of us, but also to each other. With so many, no one could really be a loner, and no one ever even thought about it. Each child was a support for the others and wanted to have that responsibility.

Barbara and I feel so fortunate that we were partners with God in having and raising our family and thank God for making it possible. We counted on Him, and He certainly came through for us.

On the subject of parents and children, I wanted to share a particularly appropriate message I heard at a funeral service in 2004 at the First Presbyterian Church of Ambler, Pennsylvania. The deceased was Evelyn Vila, the wife of Harry Vila, who had been on the Board of RSVP [an organization of senior volunteers] with me. The Reverend William J. Kemp presided, and it had to be one of the very best funeral services I have experienced.

I was so impressed with Dr. Kemp's talk that I wrote him asking him for a copy of it, and he responded favorably and quickly. Here is what he said:

One of my favorite Christian writers is the late Henri Nouwen. He was a Roman Catholic priest, and I've never met anyone who knows anything about him who hasn't been touched by the depth of his spirituality. One of his books is called "Reaching Out: The Three Movements of the Spiritual Life." The first movement is Reaching Out to Our Innermost Self – From Loneliness to Solitude; the third movement is Reaching out to God – From Illusion to Prayer; and this morning I want to lift up the second movement: Reaching Out to Our Fellow Human Beings – From Hostility to Hospitality.

Hospitality, he says, is an important Biblical concept. It "is a fundamental attitude toward our fellow human being which can be expressed in a variety of ways. Hospitality is the offer of friendship without binding the guest and freedom without leaving him alone. It is not a subtle invitation to adopt the life style of the host, but the gift of a chance for the guest to find his own."

He even applies the concept of hospitality to parents' relationships with their children. He writes, "It may sound strange to speak of the relationship between parents and children in terms of hospitality. But it belongs to the center of the Christian message that children are not properties to own and rule over, but gifts to cherish and care for. Our children are our most important guests, who enter into our home, ask for careful attention, stay for a while and then leave to follow their own way."

As I understand Nouwen, central to hospitality is the space we give to one another. Space allows us to be our own unique, individual persons. I can't do justice to his writings in a few moments, but these words from the widely read book, "The Prophet," by Kahlil Gibran help:

"Your children are not your children. They are the sons and daughters of Life's longing for itself. They come through you but not from you, and though they are with you yet they belong not to you. You may give them your love but not your souls, for their souls dwell in the house of tomorrow…You may strive to be like them, but seek not to make them like you for life goes not backward nor tarries with yesterday."

These were words that I had never heard before, and yet they sounded so logical in God's plan. I wished I had known these words back when we first started to have our family. I hope they are helpful to you, and I thank Dr. Kemp for making them available.

CHAPTER 36

A Very Enjoyable Dinner Partner

Bill Walsh is the author of this chapter.

I want to conclude by writing about the principal reason, other than my relationship with God, for any success I may have had in my adult life.

Let's say that I was a reasonably good student, self-disciplined and well organized. Fortunately, thanks to my parents and the GI Bill, I received a very good education. My friendly nature, with some help from a good golf game, allowed me to become a decent salesman. But these all pale in comparison to the importance of my being married to Barbara Straub, a very good-looking fashion model who became such a wonderful wife and mother.

We knew each other for only eight and a half months before getting married, and yet here we are, after more than six decades, very much in love and very happy with one another. When you think of the odds against this type of good fortune, you realize that God had to be behind it.

We have been so blessed that it seems almost too good to be true. Some might say they would like to have had more money than we did, but that really never seriously discouraged us. Surely we could have used money to make things easier, but it was not that important. Even if we had had more, I'm sure I still would have driven a Chevy (as I have since the early 1960s), and we'd have lived the same way.

A fancier home possibly would have been enjoyable, too, but that also wasn't important. We never wavered in our belief that once married, we were meant to love and respect one another and to welcome and love as many children as God saw fit to bless us with. That's what we believed in completely.

Barbara is probably the only woman who could ever have become my wife who would make me as happy and as close to God as I feel we are.

I thank God for bringing us together, for providing us with our family and our health for these many years, and I hope we have a few more years before we leave this earth.

I thank Barbara for being such a wonderful wife and mother—and a very enjoyable dinner partner.

FROM THE AUTHOR

Friends of Bill Walsh have told him for many years that he should write a book, that the story of the remarkable Walsh family should be set down for posterity. Bill finally agreed that the story should be told, but he did not want to be the storyteller. "I don't want to write it myself," he told me with typical candor and self-deprecation. "I don't want to come through as a big-headed Irishman who wants to look good in public." So Bill asked me to take on the assignment. I met Bill when I was reporting on his amateur golf prowess and his leadership role with the Golf Association of Philadelphia, and we became good friends. Although he was reluctant, Bill served as co-author, writing several of the chapters himself.

After nearly 30 recorded interviews with family members and friends and after poring through more than 250 typed pages of notes from Bill, this book is the result. Everyone in the family made a significant contribution, drawing from incredibly detailed remembrances dating back to childhood. Minna Walsh deserves special credit and appreciation for transcribing interviews, insisting her siblings meet deadlines and generally keeping the project on track.

The Walsh children accurately describe themselves as 15 unique individuals who love and respect each other despite sometime conflicting viewpoints. They have successfully followed 15 different paths as a great credit to the amazing people who are their parents—Bill and Barbara Walsh. It has been a joy to relate the story of the Walsh family.

Fred Behringer spent 44 years as the senior vice president and editor of a suburban Philadelphia publishing company, founded and edited golf publications in Philadelphia and New Jersey and taught communications law at Temple University. He remains active in golf communications.

MAY, 2012

APPENDICES

Walsh Open – Pine Valley Golf Club
1958 – 2007 (50 years)

PARTICIPANTS

Anthony, Jim
Anton, Fred
Arizini, Ralph
Aspen, Al *
Aspen, John *

Badgley, Gene *
Bagnell, Reds *
Balle, Bill
Bandoroff, Ben
Baroody, Tom *
Barr, Rush
Beck, Eric
Behr, Ernie *
Behringer, Fred
Bell, Dick *
Bilheimer, Harold *
Bove, Dan
Bowes, "J.B."
Brady, Jack *
Brandfass, Taylor, M.D.
Brickley, Bob
Bryant, Don *
Buccolo, Mike
Bullitt, Logan *

Burns, Jason
Burton, Bob

Carson, Bill
Carson, Jim
Charlesworth, T.J.
Coffey, Joe
Coleman, Bob *
Comerford, Jim *
Conte, Bob
Conway, Bill
Dagit, Dan
Devine, John
Dolby, Kent
Donahue, Gerry
Donahue, Gil *
Duffy, Frank
Duke, Syd *
Dunlevy, Tom

Engle, Stan
Eshelman, Jack *

Falco, Mike
Farragut, Dan

Finney, Bill
Flail, Frank
Forbes, Rick
Fowler, Martin
Frankel, Jerry
Friedman, Stan *
Funchion, Matt

Gibson, Bill
Gilhool, Ed *
Givnish, Bruce
Givnish, Tom
Goggin, Bob
Goodall, Sam *
Graff, Walter *
Grebe, Jim
Greenberg, Mike
Guidera, Jack *
Gurley, Bill

Hagerty, Joe *
Hagerty, Paul
Haley, Bob
Haley, Dan
Hallahan, Gene

Hanna, Howard
Harris, Nelson
Hausmann, Roland
Helmig, Bill *
Herman, Chuck *
Hicks, Earle
Hogan, Ned (Adm. USN)
Holloway, Cas *
Howard, Allen *
Hughes, Bill
Hurley, Harry, Jr.
Hurley, Harry, M.D. *

Imperial, Tom

Jenchura, John
Jennings, John *
Jones, Al
Jones, Bob

Kane, Charlie
Kane, Jim *
Kane, Jim, Jr.
Katz, Moe *
Katz, Morrie
Kelley, Tom *
Kelly, Bob
Kilmartin, John
Kim, Jim
Koval, George
Koval, Jack

Lamb, Jack *
Larkin, Brian
Lieberman, Jerre
Lindquist, Jay
Loftus, Bill
Logan, John
Lomorri, Bob *
Lonborg, Art
Long, Bill (Rev.)
Louderback, Lew *
Lowry, Chris

Lubker, Fred
Lundberg, Craig
Lutz, Ed

MacDonald, Bill
MacInnis, Derrick
Mansfield, Bud *
March, Bob
Marchuk, Ray
Marshall, Frank *
Marshall, Martin
Martin, Charley *
Martino, Nick
McBrien, Bill *
McCloskey, Bill
McCreavy, Joe
McCue, Charles
McEneny, Jim
McGoldrick, Ed *
McGuinn, Bill
McGuinn, John
McLellan, Jim *
Merlini, Chris
Merlini, Cornelius
Merlini, John
Merlini, Lou *
Merlini, Louis, Jr.
Merlini, Mark
Merlini, "Minnow"
Merlini, Neil
Mezzanotte, John *
Missett, Paul
Mitchell, Dick *
Moorhead, John *
Moran, Jake *
Moran, Joe
Moran, Matt
Moran, Mike
Morgan, John
Morgan, Kevin
Muldoon, Jack *
Mullen, Skip
Mundy, Bill *

Myele, Bill
Myers, Clair

Nebb, Bill *
Norris, Glen *
Noyes, Jim
O'Brien, Dave *
O'Connell, Tom *
O'Donnell, Dennis (Rev.)
O'Mara, Jack *
Orr, Bill
Ott, John *

Park, Tom *
Patrizio, Pat
Pershyn, John
Peters, Alan
Phillips, Ned *
Poole, Jack
Poore, Franny *

Queally, Frank *
Quinn, Dick

Rambo, Bob
Reich, Gil
Reimel, Ted
Rhoads, Dusty *
Riggs, George *
Riley, Mike
Robinson, Bill *
Root, Ken
Rose, Rob
Rouse, Bill
Rouse, John
Rouse, Mike

Schaeffer, Jim
Schotter, Nelson *
Schwencke, Manfred
Scott, Dick
Scott, Matt
Seelaus, Hank *

Sergovic, John
Shanahan, Ed
Shihadeh, Dave *
Siegfried, Steve
Smith, Chris
Smith, Jerry *
Snarponis, Bill
Somers, Paul *
Steele, Marty (Gen. USMC)
Steidle, Red *
Steimling, Duke *
Stieg, Fred *
Susanin, Roger

Twomey, Bob
Tracy, Dick *
Trainor, Bruce

Venuti, Rich

Waldman, Al *
Walsh, Bill
Walsh, Brendan
Walsh, Chet
Walsh, Dan
Walsh, Dave
Walsh, Matt
Walsh, Mike
Walsh, Owen *
Walsh, Tim
Warren, Ken, M.D.
Weissenberger, Erich
White, Rick *
Winslow, Hank *
Wochock, Terry
Wolfson, Merle
Wood, George

Yarnall, Steve
Yun, Dave

Zabinski, Steve

Total different participants in 50 years................225

*Deceased

Walsh Open – Pine Valley Golf Club
1958 – 2007 (50 years)

WINNERS - WALSH OPEN TROPHY

Tournament #	Year	Winner	Winner's Circle	# Wins
1-8	1958-65	NO TROPHY	Ray Marchuk	8
9	1966	John Aspen*	Joe Moran	7
10	1967	Frank Marshall*	Rick Forbes	3
11	1968	John Aspen*	John Aspen*	2
12	1969	Ned Phillips*	Buzz Heim*	2
13	1970	Joe Moran	Paul Hagerty	2
14	1971	Joe Moran	Bill Loftus	2
15	1972	John Mezzanotte	Mike Buccolo	2
16	1973	John Moorhead*	Ned Phillips*	1
17	1974	Lou Merlini*	John Mezzanotte	1
18	1975	Glenn Norris*	Lou Merlini*	1
19	1976	Dick Quinn	Glenn Norris*	1
20	1977	Buzz Heim*	Dick Quinn	1
21	1978	Jim Grebe	Jim Grebe	1
22	1979	Bill Conway	Bill Conway	1
23	1980	Joe Moran	Martin Marshall	1
24	1981	Martin Marshall	Roland Hausmann	1
25	1982	Joe Moran & Paul Hagerty	Walter Graff*	1
26	1983	Joe Moran	Stan Engle	1
27	1984	Roland Hausmann	Ed Lutz	1
28	1985	Walter Graff*	Logan Bullitt*	1
29	1986	Buzz Heim*	Brendan Walsh	1

Tournament #	Year	Winner	Winner's Circle	# Wins
30	1987	Stan Engle & Paul Hagerty	Bill McGuinn	1
31	1988	Ed Lutz	Bill Finney	1
32	1989	Bill Loftus & Logan Bullitt*	Dick Scott	1
33	1990	Bill Loftus	Bob Kelly	1
34	1991	Joe Moran	Clair Myers	1
35	1992	Ray Marchuk	Fr. Bill Long	1
36	1993	Ray Marchuk	Tim Walsh	1
37	1994	Ray Marchuk & Rick Forbes		
38	1995	Ray Marchuk		
39	1996	Joe Moran		
40	1997	Brendan Walsh		
41	1998	Bill McGuinn		
42	1999	Mike Buccolo		
43	2000	Ray Marchuk		
44	2001	Ray Marchuk		
45	2002	Ray Marchuk		
46	2003	Bill Finney & Dick Scott		
47	2004	Ray Marchuk		
48	2005	Rick Forbes, Bob Kelly, Clair Myers		
49	2006	Rick Forbes, Mike Buccolo, Fr. Bill Long		
50	2007	Tim Walsh		

*deceased

Golf Courses Played
by William T. Walsh

Arizona
Arizona – Biltmore
Scottsdale
Tatum Ranch Golf Club
Wigwam (2 courses)

California
Bermuda Dunes
California Golf Club
Canyon
Carmel Valley
Cypress Point
Del Monte
Ironwood
LaCosta
LaQuinta Country Club
Los Angeles Country Club
Marriott Course, San Diego
Olympic (Lake)
Paradise Valley
Pebble Beach
Riviera
San Diego Country Club
San Gabriel
Springs Club
Spyglass Hill
Stardust
Torrey Pines

Colorado
Broadmoor
- East
- West
- South
Cherry Hills
Fossil Trace
Vail Golf Club

Connecticut
Country Club of Fairfield
Fairview Country Club
Patterson Club
Shorehaven
Shennecossett
Stanwich
Wee Burn

Delaware
Bidermann (Vicmead)
Brandywine Country Club
Cavaliers
Deerfield Country Club
DuPont (2 courses)
Ed Oliver Golf Club
Hercules
University of Delaware
Wilmington
- North
- South

Florida

Abacoa
Adios
Admirals Cove (3 courses)
Amelia Island Plantation
Amelia National
Atlantis Country Club
Atlantis Golf Club
Ballantrae
Ballen Isles (3 courses)
Banyan
Bay Hill
Bear Lakes (2 courses)
Belleview Biltmore (2 courses)
Boca Raton Estate
Boca Raton Municipal
Boca Raton Resort (4 courses)
Bonaventure
Breakers West
Carolina Club
Cobblestone
Colony West
Coral Ridge
Country Club of Florida
Country Club of Miami
Cypress Knoll
Cypress Lakes
Delray Beach
Delray Dunes
Diplomat
Disney World
- Palm
- Magnolia
Eagle Marsh
Eagle Trace
Eastpointe
Emerald Dunes
Everglades
Fairwinds
Florida Club
Floridian
Frenchman's Creek (2 courses)
Frenchman's Reserve
Gulfstream

Hammock Creek
Hamlet Golf Club
Harbor Ridge (2 courses)
Heritage Ridge
Ibis Golf & C.C. (2 courses)
Indian Creek
Indian Pines
Indianwood
Innisbrook (2 courses)
International
Inverrary
Ironhorse
Jacaranda
John's County
John's Island (2 courses)
Jonathan's Landing (3 courses)
Jupiter Dunes
Jupiter Hills (2 courses)
Lacuna
Lake Worth
Little Club
Loblolly Pines
Lost Lake
Lost Tree Club
Loxahatchee Club
Lucerne Lakes
Madison Green
Mariner Sands (2 courses)
Mayacoo Lakes
Miami Biltmore
Mirasol (2 courses)
Mission Inn (2 courses)
Montanza Woods
Ocean Hammock
Ocean Isle
Okeeheelee
Old Marsh
Osprey Ridge
PGA National
- Champion
- Squire
- Haig
- General
PGA Village (2 courses)

Palm Beach Country Club
Palm Beach National
Palm Cove
Pine Lakes
Pine Tree
Plantation
Poinciana
Ponce de Leon
Ponte Vedra (2 courses)
Quail Ridge (2 courses)
Red Stick
River Bend (Ormond Beach)
Riverbend (Tequesta)
Rolling Hills
Sailfish Point
Savanna Club
Sawgrass
Seminole
St. Augustine Shores
Summer Beach
Summerfield
TPC Sawgrass (2 courses)
Tequesta
Tesoro
Turtle Bay (67)
Turtle Creek
Village Green
West Palm Beach C.C.
West Palm Beach Polo
Westchester Country Club
Winston Trails
Wycliffe

Georgia
Atlanta Athletic Club
Augusta
Deer Creek
Sea Island (4 courses)
The Landings - Skidaway
    Island (5 courses)

Hawaii
Kaanapali (2 courses)

Kapalua
- Bay
- Village
Mauna Kea
Mauna Lani
Oahu Country Club
Pearl Country Club
Waialae Country Club
Wailea
- Blue
- Orange

Illinois
Chicago Golf Club

Louisiana
Lakewood Golf Club

Maine
Webhannet

Maryland
Baltimore C.C. (Five Farms)
Caves Valley
Columbia
Congressional
Eagles Landing
Forest Park
Ocean Pines
Woodholme

Massachusetts
Charles River
Oyster Harbors
Ponkapoag
Salem
Sankaty Head
The Country Club
Weston

Missouri
Kansas City C.C.
    (1985 Rotary)

Nevada
Las Vegas Country Club

New Jersey
Allaire
Ash Brook Golf Club
Atlantic City
Avalon
Baltusrol (2 courses)
Ballamor
Battleground
Blue Heron Pines
Bowling Green
Braidburn
Burlington
Canoe Brook (2 courses)
Cedar Hill
Colonia
Copper Hill
Deal
Deerwood
East Orange
Echo Lake
Essex County
Essex County West
Essex Fells
Flanders Valley
Forest Hill Field Club
Forsgate
Galloping Hill
Galloway
Greenacres
Hidden Creek
Hollywood
Homestead
Hopewell Valley
Hydewood
Jasna Polana
Knoll Golf Club
Lakewood
Laurel Creek
Laurence Brook
Links

Little Mill
Locust Grove
Manasquan River
Maple Ridge
Medford Lakes
Medford Village
Metedeconk
Metuchen (64-CR)
Montclair (2 courses)
Moorestown Field Club
Morris County
Netherwood
Nomahegan
North Jersey Country Club
Oak Ridge (67-CR)
Old Orchard
Olde York
Penn Brook
Pennsauken
Pine Valley (73) (2 courses)
Pine Hill
Plainfield (69)
Plainfield West
Playboy Club
Preakness Hills
Rancocas Golf Club
Raritan Valley
Ridgewood (2 courses)
Riverton
Rock Spring
Rossmoor
Rumson
Running Deer
Rutgers
Sand Barrens
Scotland Run
Seaview (2 courses)
Shackamaxon
Somerset Hills
Spring Brook
Spring Lake
Spring Meadow
Springdale

Stone Harbor
Suburban
Sunnyfield
Sunset Valley
Tavistock
Teaneck
Trenton
Twin Brooks (69)
Twisted Dune
Upper Montclair
White Beeches
Woodbury
Woodcrest

New York
Bonnie Briar
Concord
Country Club of Rochester
Garden City
Grossinger (2 courses)
Lake Placid
LaTourette
Lido
Long Island National
Metropolis
Mohonk Mountain House
Montauk Downs
National
Oak Hill
Purchase Country Club
Richmond County
Sagamore
Shinnecock
St. George's
Tallgrass
Westchester
Winged Foot
- ▪ East
- ▪ West

North Carolina
Beau Rivage
Biltmore Forest

Country Club of Asheville
Brierwood
Cape Golf Club
Grove Park Inn
Hickory Meadow
Magnolia Greens
Ocean Isle
Stonebridge

Ohio
Muirfield
The Golf Club
Trumbull Country Club

Pennsylvania
ACE
Applebrook
Applecross
Aronimink (70)
Arrowhead
Ashbourne
Bala (68)
Bedford Springs
Bella Vista
Bent Creek
Berkleigh
Berkshire
Blue Bell
Brookside Allentown
Brookside Pottstown
Cedarbrook (New)
Cedarbrook (Old)
Center Square
Chester Valley (New)
Chester Valley (Old)
Coatesville
Cobbs Creek
Commonwealth
Concord
Country Club of York
Downingtown
Doylestown
Eagle Lodge

Eagles Mere
Earlington Park
Edgmont
Flourtown
Franklin D. Roosevelt
Galen Hall
General Washington
   (Shannondell)
Gilbertsville
Glenhardie
Glenmaura
Glen Mills
Golden Oaks
Green Valley
Grove City
Gulph Mills
Hartefeld
Heidelberg
Hershey C.C. (2 courses)
Hershey Hotel
Hershey Park
Hershey's Mill
Hickory Valley (2 courses)
Honeybrook
Horsham Valley
Host Farms - Downingtown
Host Farms- Lancaster
Huntingdon Valley (2)
Huntsville
Indian Valley
Inniscrone
Jeffersonville
John F. Byrne
Juniata
Karakung
Kennett Square
Kimberton
Lancaster Country Club
Lehigh
Limekiln
Limerick
Llanerch
Lookaway

Lulu Temple
Main Line (69)
Manufacturers
McCall Field
Meadowbrook
Meadowlands
Melrose
Merion
- East (71)
- West
Middletown
Moselem Springs
Mount Airy
Mountain Laurel
North Hills
Northampton - Easton
Northampton Valley
Oakmont
Oak Terrace
Old York Road (New)
Old York Road (Old)
Olde Masters
Overbrook
Paxon Hollow
Penn Oaks
Philadelphia Cricket (2 courses)
Philadelphia Country Club
- Spring Mill (65)
- Centennial
Philmont (2 courses)
Phoenixville
Pine Crest
Pittsburgh Field Club
Plymouth
Pocono Manor (2 courses)
Radley Run
Radnor Valley
Raven's Claw
Reading
Rolling Green
Rolling Turf
Sandy Run

Saucon Valley
- ▪ Old
- ▪ Grace
- ▪ Weyhill

Seven Springs
Shawnee
Silver Creek
Skippack
Skytop
Split Rock Lodge
Springfield
Spring-Ford
Springhaven (69)
Spring Hollow
Spring Mill
Squires
St. Davids
Stonewall (2 courses)
Sunnybrook
Talamore
Tamiment
Tattersall
Torresdale-Frankford
Valley Forge
Venango
Walnut Lane
Waynesborough
West Chester
Westover
White Manor
Whitemarsh
Whitford
Williamsport
Woodloch Springs
Woodstone
Worcester
Wyncote
Yardley

South Carolina
Camden
Charleston National
Hidden Cypress

Indian Wells
Lady's Island
Lake Marion
Long Cove
Ocean Creek
Ocean Point
Okatie
River Oaks
Rivers-Bend
Santee Cooper
Santee National
Whispering Pines
Wild Dunes (2 courses)
Wyboo

Texas
Forest Creek
River Place

Virginia
Birdwood
Cavalier
Country Club of Virginia
Golden Horseshoe
Homestead (3)
Kingsmill
Princess Anne
Red Wing
Roanoke
Virginia Beach
Washington G & CC
Williamsburg

West Virginia
Greenbrier (3 courses) (69)
Lakeview

Outside the United States

Bermuda
Castlen Harbor
Mid-Ocean
Southampton Princess

Nassau
Bahamas Princess
Kings Inn

Puerto Rico
Berwind
Cerromar (2 courses)
Dorado Beach (2 courses)
El Conquistador

Scotland
Airdrie (final round)
Carnoustie
Gleneagles - Kings
Prestwick
Royal Troon
St. Andrews
Old
New
Turnberry - Ailsa

Ireland
Adare Manor
Ardglass
Ballybunion (New)
Ballybunion (Old)
Connemara
County Louth (Baltray)
Dooks
Enniscrone
Island Club
Killarney
- Killeen
- Mahoney

Lahinch
Portmarnock
Royal Portrush
Royal County Down
Royal Dublin
Sligo (Rosses Point)
Tralee
Waterville

PAST LOYALTY AWARD RECIPIENTS

Presented for Unending Loyalty, Throughout the Years, to Villanova

Year	Awardee	Class	Year	Awardee	Class
			* 1971	Rev. Edward McKee, OSA	'28
* 1932	Charles A. McGeehan	'12	* 1972	Samuel J. Canning, Jr.	'47
* 1933	J. Stanley Smith, Esq.	'93	* 1973	Edward D. Riley	'43
* 1934	Martin J. McLaughlin	'14	* 1974	Nicholas L. Caruso	'35
* 1935	Thomas M. Dalton	'12	* 1975	John J. McAndrews	'30
* 1936	James P. Leaming	'10	* 1976	Arthur L. Mahan	'36
* 1937	F. Leo Lynch	'16	1977	Thomas J. Burke	'49
* 1938	M. Eugene Eichman	'14	* 1978	James F. Haughton	'41
* 1939	Cyril J. Burke	'17	* 1979	Thomas F. Devine, Esq.	'43
* 1940	John B. Keffer	'25	1980	Jacques E. Mauch	'43
* 1941	John J. Dougherty	'18	* 1981	William J. Bradley	'31
* 1942	Edward J. Burke, Ph.D.	'23	1982	Ronald F. Russo, MD	'52
* 1943	Michael P. Fogarty, DDS	'18	* 1983	Thomas J. Morgan	'31
* 1944	Francis X. Robinson	'21	* 1984	Douglas J. Murray	'61
* 1945	Charles H. McGuckin	'18	1985	Donald R. Creamer	'70
* 1946	Matthew A. Lynch	'23	1986	Richard N. Winfield, Esq.	'55
* 1947	Hon Theodore L. Reimel	'24	* 1987	William H. Vincent, Jr.	'60
* 1948	William M. Connelly	'27	1988	John F. Heilmann	'49
* 1949	Martin L. Gill	'32	1989	Frank J. Miller	'59
* 1950	Joseph D. Freney, Esq.	'27	1990	Charles W. Johnson '63	
* 1951	M. L. Caine, Sr., Esq.	'04	* 1991	William G. McDonnell	'49
* 1952	Paetrus F. Banmiller	'35	1992	Robert J. Capone	'62
* 1953	William H. Vincent, Esq.	'28	* 1993	Arthur M. Blanche	'49
* 1954	David F. Farley	'20	1994	James W. Eastwood	'68
* 1955	Joseph P. Deluca	'30	1995	George W. Piper	'67

Year	Awardee	Class	Year	Awardee	Class
* 1956	William B. Sheehan	'25	1996	Martin F. Whalen	'63
* 1957	James F. Elliott	'35	1997	James G. O'Connor	'64
* 1958	James P. Quindlen, MD	'28	1998	Joseph C. Hare, Esq.	'72
* 1959	Marshall J. Halphen	'27	1999	Alvin A. Clay	'51
* 1960	Alex G. Severance	'29	2000	Michael P. Manning	'69
* 1961	Joseph E. Walters	'45	* 2001	Joseph J. Manion	'61
* 1962	Daniel L. Redmond, Sr.	'17	2002	Louis R. Kahl	'55
* 1963	William C. Henry, Esq.	'25	2003	William J. Fallon	'67
* 1964	W.E. Schubert, Jr., Esq.	'42	* 2004	Carol Donoghue	'72
* 1965	John A. White	'09	* 2005	Joseph T. Mooney, Jr.	'56
* 1966	Edward J. Donahue	'33	2006	Francis H. Dunne, Esq.	'64
* 1967	William C. Faulk	'30	2007	Howard Long	'82
1968	William T. Walsh	'43	2008	Judy Lee Burke Brooks	'75
* 1969	C. Edward Burnshaw	'32	2009	Edward J. Welsh	'66
* 1970	Patrick J. Romano, MD	'30	2010	James Magee	'75
			2011	Harold A. Jensen	'87

* Deceased